Fritham
An Ancient New Forest Village

The history of a unique New Forest village through the centuries

Edited by
Hugh Pasmore
Margaret Houlgate
Marie Heinst

2000

ISBN 0952583445

Printed by Ensign Press, Southern Road, Southampton. Hampshire SO15 1HA

FOREWORD

In this Millennium Year thousands of villages throughout the land will be marking the event in special ways. But surely Fritham, a New Forest village with an idyllic setting, has chosen the best way of commemorating its survival: documenting by word and picture many of the colourful characters who have lived within its bounds, as well as the events in which they played a part.

The one thread running throughout Fritham's story is its association with the Forest. Indeed, its very name (roughly translated) says it all - a settlement amongst the trees. Its island location in the Forest meant that the early inhabitants were dependent on each other for their existence. It meant, too, that they had to be expert in extracting the best from the soil and woodland about them. Indeed those ancient needs are today encompassed in the Rights of the Commoner.

"There is nothing permanent except change," runs an old adage. Fritham has not escaped the effect of change, good or bad. Historians have recorded such incidents as violence amongst royal huntsmen, imposition of cruel taxes, smuggling, illegal killing of Forest animals and felling of Forest trees. But with the arrival of the 19th century there came a wealth of firsthand accounts by villagers detailing everyday life in Fritham. These true stories extend right up to the present and include the Second World War, arguably the most significant event of the last century.

Varied and vividly recounted, these accounts often evoke nostalgia for bygone days of the village shop, post office, church, school and pub. Today, sadly, only the church and The Royal Oak remain from these former village institutions.

Yet the people of Fritham, though bereft of much that was useful in the past, vigorously sustain the village's identity with a fierce determination to carry on in the future. With the same spirit of "Love thy neighbour as thyself" documented so tellingly in these pages, the future of the village must surely be assured for millenniums to come.

James Mays

ACKNOWLEDGEMENTS

Our thanks to all the villagers of Fritham, past and present who helped us to gather the significant and interesting information within this book. It is their creative contributions that have added character and originality to our efforts.

We are particularly grateful to Jude James from Wessex Educational Services for his advice and guidance as we researched the historical evidence for Chapter Two. Jude helped us to present our findings in a more acceptable and rigorous format. Any historical mistakes are entirely unintentional. We are also grateful to Anthony Pasmore for providing the account of Fritham's Unwritten History.

A special thank you to Edwina Bright (nee Batten) who supplied a number of excellent photographs to illustrate places, people and events in Fritham. Edwina also helped us to secure further information concerning past events in Fritham. Our thanks also to her brother Alf Batten for providing such vivid memories of living in Fritham. We would also like to acknowledge the advice provided by Dennis Bush particularly in respect of the war years in Fritham.

We appreciate the help given by Carl Heinst in typing some of our material and preparing the chapters for the printers.

Finally, we are delighted that James Mays agreed to write the Foreword to our book.

CONTENTS

OUR VILLAGE

In the north west corner of the New Forest, a stone's throw from the Wiltshire border, nestles the ancient village of Fritham, a hamlet of less than 200 people. It was an area known to Stone and Bronze Age man, and long before the Jutes and Saxons settled there, the Romans exploited the resources by making pottery. Archaeologists regularly search the Forest floor for Roman pottery, and findings of Georgian coins. The remains of Victorian bottles and modern Elizabethan beer cans can point to a continuation of settlements for many hundreds of years.

Fritham, although part of Bramshaw parish, was always (and remains) an isolated island settlement in the Forest and consequently has remained remarkably independent in the conduct of its affairs. The name Fritham most probably comes from Frith-ham, where Frith means a scrubby woodland or coppice, and referred at that time to the timber and branches that were brought from it.

1. Fritham - an old picture postcard circa early 1900's

For generations this small village slept at the end of the track which disappeared into the silent forest. Most farmsteads kept a few cows, pigs and hens on an acre or two and villagers came together to help each other with the harvesting. Fields rang with the sound of scythes, and cider with hunks of bread and cheese, brought to the fields by the women, kept spirits high until the horse drawn wagons took weary bodies home.

Many of the old cottages had Forest Rights, granted from a Register of Claims in 1670, and given statutory recognition in the 1698 Act. The Rights entitled the owners or tenants to collect an allocation of wood, to cut turf and depasture their animals. Pannage rights allowed pigs to forage for acorns in the Autumn time, for a variable period depending on the crop of acorns, thus preventing the ponies from eating too many, a diet which too often proved fatal. Some of these Rights such as estovers and turbary belong to the hearth of the cottage, but other Rights such as pannage belong to the property in general such as a field without a building.

The children grew up knowing where to find the primroses, violets and wood anemones and which dangerous bogs to avoid. They knew the secret places of the shy orchids and wild gladioli, and brought home arms full of bluebells.

Today, although much is unchanged in the glades and marshlands, and animals still graze the green and wander down the lanes, life in Fritham has changed. Car park barriers, across the once peaceful tracks and dragons' teeth to protect the Forest from the high volume of cars of visitors who have 'discovered' Fritham, have become part of the landscape. The foxhounds still, for the time being, meet on the green as do the beagles. It is also the venue for Adventure Scouts, orienteering, treasure hunts, hikers and bikers. Pony and trap clubs rumble through the lanes, barrels are rolled and Morris Dancers entertain, while hot air balloons sigh overhead. Weekends see crowds of people enjoying the beauty where once the rustle of leaves and the cry of a bird were the only signs of life.

The local flora is not unique to Fritham and mirrors that of other parts of the Forest, but many rare orchids and wild gladioli together with butterflies, yellowhammers and larks have sadly disappeared from the glades where they once abounded.

The Forest enfolding Fritham doesn't change though. Shaded by the dense foliage, sunlit glades and the sparkling streams, the trees have a timeless quality about them. While the deer, fox and badger roam under the huge oaks and Bronze Age barrows lie undisturbed on Fritham Plain, the village lives on.

CHAPTER ONE - IN THE BEGINNING

Fritham's Unwritten History

Exactly when Fritham's fields were enclosed out of the Open Forest is unknown. It used to be said that the village possessed several entries in the Domesday Book, but recent research confirms that these relate to a farm in Boldre Hundred and now on the Beaulieu Estate.

Eyeworth, as Ivare, does have its own entry. The first certain reference to Fritham proper would seem to be in the early 13th Century - over a hundred years after Domesday. No archaeological fieldwork has been undertaken within the village itself and we are not aware of any finds which have been made in the past, with the exception of a brick kiln (see below). The origin of the village is thus entirely obscure. We do, however, know a good deal about the archaeology of the Forest surrounding Fritham and the area which the village now occupies may be assumed to have had a similar prehistory.

The first widespread evidence of human occupation of the New Forest is from the Mesolithic period (about 5000 to 12000 years ago). The waste material from the production of flint tools is found scattered almost everywhere, with one of the most important manufactories locally being in King's Garn Gutter Inclosure. Very much later, in the Bronze Age (2500 to nearly 4000 years ago), the Forest was probably just beginning to evolve its present heathland vegetation. A number of communal water-heating sites were then established on spring lines around Fritham. These 'boiling troughs' are known to exist near North Bentley and Queen's North Wood. The Bronze Age people were also sufficiently settled to construct circular burial mounds called barrows or tumuli. Surviving examples are to be seen at The Butt near Moor Cottage, around Hiscocks Hill and near Eyeworth.

In the Iron Age (2000 to 2500 years ago) more permanent farming started in the area with small agricultural holdings at Dark Hat, near Eyeworth and possibly in Sloden Wood and Sloden Inclosure. Occupation into the Roman period was then probably continuous. Important pottery making industries developed in the woods north west of Fritham. A supposed branch Roman road was made from Stoney Cross. It can be traced into the village near New Farm, but where it went after that is uncertain.

In the post-Roman period, the archaeology of the Fritham area is more obscure. Coppice enclosures, from which the original banks may still be seen, were made at North and South Bentley and were certainly in existence in Elizabethan times. Charcoal burning by the traditional pit method continued up to the early years of this century and abandoned pits may be seen in Suburbs Wood, on Fritham Plain and in Howen Bottom.

The village itself was almost certainly larger at one time with remains of abandoned fields visible near Fritham Lodge, west of Janesmoor House and (probably) near Fritham House. There is no evidence as to the date of these enclosures, but similar abandoned fields in other parts of the Forest are known to be of 17th and 18th Century origin.

Within Fritham itself, the only archaeological feature so far recorded is the site of a brick kiln of unknown date in the field called Puncherdons near the old village pound.

CHAPTER TWO

Centuries of Change

Fritham in old English parlance, 'A settlement among the trees,' has a history spanning many centuries and in the peat in Fritham woods will be found the decaying rings of Plantagenet, Tudor, Stuart and Hanoverian trees.

While William and Harold fought at Hastings, Henry II caused Becket's murder and John signed the Magna Carta, the thatchers and ditchers of Fritham were going about their daily business. Did they know of Edward II's defeat at Bannockburn, the 100 years war with France or the Black Death, while they collected firewood and cultivated their fields? And did travellers ever bring news to the isolated village of young Edward V's murder in the Tower, the dramas of Henry VIII's reign, or the true glories of Elizabeth I's years?

We shall never know how much or how little the people of Fritham knew about the world outside the Forest, but we can examine some of our research findings to try to make sense of Fritham's development through the centuries.

11th and 12th Centuries

What we do know is that Fritham was a favourite hunting ground of the early kings, with the exception of Henry I, who remembering his brother Rufus's unfortunate accident with an arrow always gave the Forest a wide berth.

13th and 14th Centuries - The Bailiwick of Fritham:

In the thirteenth century Fritham was one of six bailiwicks. A bailiwick was an area under the jurisdiction of a bailiff. The villagers of Fritham lived under forest law as well as the common law all people were bound by. Offences committed under forest law included capturing and taking sparrowhawks from the Fritham area and the removal of Fritham oak trees. The former offence present day villagers may overlook, the latter they are still vigilant in protecting.

There was a hunting lodge at Eyeworth, and the history of Fritham Lodge points to that house also being a favourite with royalty. Not that these lodges had much in common with the present day buildings. They were probably of puddled clay bound together with layers of heather, and thatched roofs to keep them dry. In Studley Wood, there is an earthwork known as Studley Castle. This is the site of one of the later royal Hunting Lodges and was built around 1360 in Edwards III's reign, when England was recovering from the terrible effects of the Black Death. The Lodge was timber framed and roofed with Cornish or Purbeck slates and had a surrounding ditch. The Lodge provided overnight accommodation for hunting parties. A similar lodge also existed in Church Place, Old Sloden.

Commoners' Rights came into being as a compensation for not being able to fence their land against the hunt, and instead they were allowed to depasture their animals on the Forest, dig turf and in some cases take an allocation of wood. A valuation of land in Fritham around the 1300's revealed a total of 67 acres attributed to fourteen villagers. Present day Fritham has 330 acres and approximately 125 villagers.

In 1327 a total of twenty-six shillings, six and three quarter pence was collected from nine taxpayers in 'Frytham' and 'Cantertone'. This was a government tax assessed at one-twentieth of the value on moveable property.

15th Century

Over 600 years ago Fritham tempted clergy, gentlemen and villagers to fall foul of forest laws. In 1485 one Thomas Rypon of Plaitford, entered Fritham with greyhounds and killed a doe and carried away the flesh without permission. In the January of the same year Robert Bulkeley and William Kaylleway with bows and arrows as well as greyhounds, killed 5 fawns, 1 doe and a pricket. In 1492 Sir William Holme a priest of Salisbury killed a 'sore' with his greyhounds, without seeking the permission of the keeper. There is no record of the punishments for these deeds, which for a few cruel years after the creation of the Forest might have been blinding, amputation of hands or even death. However, a mutilated man was a liability and an expense, whereas a fine would represent an income. According to Stagg I, 'there is evidence in the Pipe Roll of 31 Henry I (1131) that at that time venison offenders were being punished by means of a fine.'

16th Century

We may complain of taxes, but they have always been with us and in 1586 Elizabeth authorised the collection of a further lay subsidy. This was a grant to the Crown, authorised by an Act of Parliament, to create a tax to support necessary expenditure, including payment of the forces and the building of naval ships. The Clergy was subjected to a separate assessment. The tax was based on the valuation of a person's moveable goods, including crops, which was levied at one fifteenth on rural dwellers. Ten residents of Fritham had goods valued at £3 to £5, and tax to the value of 37 shillings was collected.

17th Century

Illegal hunting in Fritham was not the only crime committed during the 17th century. The prize for persistence must go to Mr Gabriel Lapp esquire of Fritham who first came to the notice of the courts on the 1st May 1628, when he went over the top and cut and felled 55 decayed oaks worth £12. He was fined £10. He obviously thought he was on to a profitable activity, and regular appearances in court for at least a further 7 years record that he felled on various occasions 40, 50, 86 and a staggering 216 oaks. Between 1628 and 1636 he felled something over 700 trees, mainly decayed oaks. The fines were always below the value of the trees.

In 1634, Arthur Oxford gent of Fritham, cut and lopped various trees (worth £6) to sell for his advantage rather than for the necessary forage for his stock. This incurred a fine of £5. Interesting to note 'a gun loaded with powder and lead' was used by a yeoman from Cadnam to kill a buck near Ocknell in 1660.

We have a little more information about the folk of Fritham, from the Hearth Tax Assessment of 1665. The tax was introduced in 1662 to alleviate Charles II's financial difficulties. An annual tax of two shillings payable on every firehearth or stove within all dwellings, houses, edifices or lodgings, was collected in two instalments, on Michaelmas, 29th September and Lady Day, 25th March.

The first payment of this tax was collected in 1662, and continued for 27 years until 1689 when it was abolished following the 1688 revolution, as one of the first acts of William and Mary. It was replaced by the Window Tax. Fritham at this time was a well-populated and warm village as 103 hearths were taxed, an increase of 24 over the previous year. Some homes were warmer than others, and owners ranged from widow Hoare with 1 hearth, to Mister Richard Bassett and Mister John Aldridge with a heartwarming 6 each. There was exemption for the very poor, however, and 29 homes worth less than £1 were exempt.

It would appear Fritham was a village of extremes some 300 years ago, with some dwellings worth as little as 6d per annum such as a cottage with garden and orchard and an adjacent piece of land called Crowders containing 5 acres. A cottage still stands on the site. At the other end of the scale we see that claims were made on the New Forest for rights of pasture, pannage etc.

At that time eight houses were registered to five Fritham villagers in the Book of Claims:

Edmund Yeoman 1 house and 5 acres
John Emblym 2 houses, 17 acres and 3 hearths
Andrew Elliot 3 houses and 59 acres
John Cooke 1 house and 10 acres
Edward Acton 1 house and 50 acres

Stagg 15th - 17th Centuries Book of Claims 1670

18th Century

Smugglers' Tales

When considering smuggling, we must remember that although it would appear it was for some years important in Fritham, it was an illegal and therefore secret activity. Over the years many romantic and often unsubstantiated stories have been passed down to us. In order to understand Fritham's role in this activity the reader may find it helpful to have the following background information.

Geographically speaking, the New Forest was an ideal location for smuggling in the eighteenth and nineteenth centuries. The English South coast faced the shores of France from whence most of the contraband came and illicit cargo could be taken into the Forest, sorted and be on its way within minutes.

This 'free-trading' was big business and played a very important part in the life of the New Forest community during these centuries. Taxation was severe, a labourer's wage was 7 shillings and 6 pence a week, and any opportunity to ease the poverty was willingly taken. These 'Gentlemen of the Night' were prepared to risk transportation or hanging for 2 shillings and 6 pence a keg for a night's smuggling.

Smuggling was a game of cat and mouse, involving nearly everybody in the community, with the squire or Venturer providing the capital and local traders, doctor and even the parson taking an active part, or turning a blind eye. It is wrong to imagine that smuggling was carried on by a few desperate individuals; on the contrary they were an organised band of farm workers, tradesmen, fishermen and workers in various trades. As few of these folk could read or write, there had to be a scribe or secretary who organised the proceedings and kept records of the activities.

There were also women who enjoyed the excitement and took an active part in the smuggling, either joining in the contraband run or acting as look out. Lovey Warne was one such who joined with her brothers Peter and John on the contraband run, but her main task was to wear a cloak of brightest scarlet and stand at Picket Post as a warning that Abram Pike, the Riding Officer in 1803, was abroad.

The smugglers greatly outnumbered the Revenue Officers who, coming face to face with a large band of determined men, often decided to turn a blind eye. Jokes were exchanged together with a few kegs, and each party continued on its way in a mood of mutual satisfaction.

Chewton Bunny, the outlet for Chewton Glen at Christchurch Bay, was a perfect landing place for the brandy, tea, silks and other contraband. The

Bunny extends well into the New Forest and was an excellent Smugglers' Way in the direction of Burley. Much has been written about the part played by The Queen's Head at Burley, and the Cat and Fiddle Inn at Hinton during the smuggling years, but the Royal Oak at Fritham can also tell a tale.

Contraband would be brought in wagons or on horseback to The Cat and Fiddle, where it was loaded by willing hands, both men and girls, on to ponies with sacks over their backs. According to old records, these goods would be taken 'through Vereley and Ridley up to Smugglers' Road and on to Fritham'.

One of the tales told of those days involves a smugglers' ship that was caught and towed into Poole Harbour and the crew thrown into goal. Their forest friends hearing of their plight gathered reinforcements at Lyndhurst, and rode up to Fritham where, at the Royal Oak they refreshed themselves for the night ahead. They then slipped quietly through Amberwood, Sloden and into Poole.

They overpowered the guards, rescued the smugglers and loaded up the contraband before making their getaway. Unfortunately, they stopped at the George Inn at Fordingbridge and tarried too long to celebrate their victory, because soldiers and Customs Officers caught up with them and a battle took place in Bridge Street. Some smugglers paid with their lives, but the ringleaders escaped with much of the contraband.

Some of the captured smugglers were 'persuaded' to turn coats, and they were released after they had revealed that their companions would take refuge at Frogham and Fritham. However, news through the Forest telegraph warned the gang of this treachery, and they ambushed the turncoats, beat them to death and buried them on the Bramshaw Ridge. It is said that the tale does not have a happy ending for the rest of the smugglers either, as they were eventually rounded up and hanged in chains - some at Fritham.

19th Century

In the middle of the 19th Century the inhabitants of Fritham engaged in a variety of occupations. A number of villagers were labourers, carriers and carpenters. Most of the registered names are no longer familiar to present day villagers with the exception of the name Thorne and some traditional 'Forest' names such as Cordery, Henbest and Deacon. In the 19th century Thorne and Cordrey were shopkeepers and Fielder a boot and shoemaker in Fritham. Parnell and Spratt were farmers with farmer Miller also registered as a shopkeeper. Jefferies and Smith tended smallholdings and a number of villagers were cowkeepers. Another Miller was recorded as a timber measurer. A teacher of music called Spence provided an additional area of expertise within the village.

2. The Royal Oak at the beginning of the 20th century

The Royal Oak had at least three different licensees during the 19th century a G.F. Bowles in 1859, Robert Andrews in 1878, and Daniel Bessant in 1895. A gardener called Tugby lived and worked in the village. Fritham also boasted two esquires called Munro and Strange, and two gentlemen called Thomas Chitty and John Montagu. While Admiral Heathcote lived in the splendour of Fritham Lodge and Mr R.W.S. Griffiths, a well-known chemist resided in Eyeworth Lodge, a number of less fortunate villagers were recorded as living 'under canvas'. These folk lived in rather makeshift dwellings in the Forest around Fritham, earning a living by making chairs or in some cases the occupation was recorded as 'a wanderer'. These makeshift dwellings were used by folk willing to move swiftly in search of short-term work.

1891 Census Returns
1859 Kelly's Trade Directory

Early 20th Century

Jesse Taylor's Diary

Jesse Taylor was a New Forest Agister within the Fritham area from 1907 to 1923. In 1877 the Court of Verderers of the New Forest had been reconstituted to regulate and control the exercise of common rights; and in the opinion of the Verderers, to act as guardians of the Forest and as a watchdog of the Crown's silvicultural and estate management objectives. The agisters were appointed by the Court of Verderers to deal with the practical administration of the Verderers' authority in guarding the Forest. Among the early 'Instructions to Agisters' (1887 Edition) is one item of particular relevance to the diary:

> *'17. Each Agister shall keep a Memorandum Book (to be supplied by the Verderers) in which he shall enter, with the date, any enquiry made by a commoner or Non-Commoner as to animals marked by him, and the result of such enquiry.'*

It is probable that this instruction remained substantially unchanged in Jesse Taylor's day, and may well have given rise to the diary. The diary gives a unique picture of the everyday life of a New Forest Commoner. Jesse spent the first part of his life in Burley before moving to 'The Tea House' at Picket Post in 1910. His job was the great interest of his life and he worked six days a week, usually riding at least 20 miles a day, often very much more, in all weathers, summer and winter. He was totally dependent upon his horse and bicycle to carry out his duties as agister.

In the course of his duties a typical day would involve Jesse leaving Picket Post travelling to '*...Woodgreen and Godshill colt marking came back and had a look over Ashley Hills for Mr. Pinhorn's mare and colt. Could not find them but saw seven red deer near Ashley. I came on by the Telegraph (Hill) and by Fritham round Stoney Cross way...*' before reaching home.

His diary logs successful colt hunting using his bicycle and helped by a few other commoners. Messages were relayed to Jesse in various forms including the use of telegrams. In 1913 he received a telegram from H. Winter of Fritham informing him of a mare who had gone down on Longcross Plain. He witnessed and recorded many interesting events in his diary including troop manoeuvres over Stoney Cross Plain in 1914. Jesse's entry for March 19th. 1923 (the final year of his diary) makes reference to the ruins of the Gunpowder Factory at Eyeworth Lodge '*Went to Fritham and marked some colts at the Powder Mills whilst there the Deer Hounds killed a Buck inside on the Factory ruins.*'

The diary also traces the changing pattern of smallholding economics. In the early days Jesse is cutting turf for fuel, while in the latter years he goes to Burley for coal. Throughout the greater part of his time he cuts fern for bedding, but in the latter years (1920's) he uses straw. The Forest of Jesse's day was already threatened by the motor vehicle.

Jesse Taylor's Diary 1907- 1923

CHAPTER THREE

In Living Memory

Bygone Days in Fritham by Hugh Pasmore

I came to live in Fritham village in 1933 and have seen it 'advance' from virtually no modern conveniences until today when it boasts all modern amenities. Before the 1939 war many cottages had their own wells from which water was drawn in a bucket, usually assisted by some form of pulley with which the filled bucket was raised to the surface. Often in the summer wells would run dry and then we had to journey to the other end of the village, beyond the Royal Oak and on to Little Green Pond where a first class unfailing spring supplied unlimited clear water. This still remains in full flow and until quite recently one villager insisted on using it to dilute his whisky. Those who were fortunate enough to own a pony and cart collected their spring water in a variety of containers, frequently milk churns. Some children trundled a hand truck or wheelbarrow, which carried various types of containers - this involved quite a journey but was accepted as a matter of course and not regarded as a burden. I had bought the White House at the other end of the village, and being in business had no time for such trips, so when our well ran dry, Joe Payne, the Emery Down builder sank an 18 foot well which never failed in twenty years.

Earth closets were of course universal and were usually discreetly situated at the bottom of the garden.

Lighting was another problem and depended very much on one's financial position. The few large houses such as Fritham House, a fairly recently built country house, had electricity generating engines, but the majority of cottages were dependent on artificial light in the way of candles, simple single or double burner oil lamps or hurricane lamps (used for outside the house). A little more costly but giving excellent illumination, were Aladdin lamps, which were fuelled by paraffin and had mantles; these gave excellent lighting but were subject to sudden fits of sooty black smoking if unattended. For outside lighting as well as the hurricane lamp a more sophisticated pressure lamp was introduced called Tilley lamps. This variety of lamps was most important where farms and smallholdings were concerned for in winter the evening milking was invariably after dark.

Transport in the 1930's was something of a problem for though the motor car had become commonplace the cost was high. Farmers were not badly off for they already had their horses and carts. Others had to depend on the bicycle or local bus which latter was rather infrequent and when coming through Nomansland sometimes found it necessary to lighten its load by disembarking its passengers at the foot of Pipers Wait Hill while it travelled to the summit unencumbered, and resumed its journey when the passengers reached the top on foot and re-embarked. I had a fairly ancient Morris Cowley car in which I travelled daily to Lyndhurst and frequently I did shopping for villagers. One thing especially required constant attention - the re-charging of the wireless batteries.

Television had not then arrived and we all relied on battery wireless sets. These worked in conjunction with an outdoor aerial suspended normally between your roof and the nearest tree. The battery charge lasted for about 2 weeks and I had a regular run having them recharged in Lyndhurst for various neighbours. A few people made do with the crystal sets which required no battery but entailed the use of headphones and a delicate wire which had to be contacted with a crystal - generally most unsatisfactory.Cooking and water heating also presented problems. Of the many variety of oil cookers the most popular seemed to be Florence and Valors, some still had coal burning iron ranges which also heated water. About the same time Calor gas stoves became popular and for the wealthier households Agas made their appearance but at £100 few could afford the luxury.

The village had no rubbish collection but the powers that be allocated an old gravel pit amidst the hollies in Howen Bushes just beyond the Royal Oak where we were permitted to dump our rubbish. This functioned well enough and I don’t remember it being abused in any way.

There was little in the way of entertainment for the younger generation in the village, but teenagers thought nothing of bicycling to Ringwood, Fordingbridge, Romsey and even Southampton to see a film. For the very young Miss Stubbs at Woodland Cottage near the Royal Oak ran a club known as the Happy Chums club whilst, Gerald Forward at Valletta House in winter had weekly whist parties.

Employment in the village depended to a large extent on farming. The principal farmers were the Hickman brothers at New Farm, Bert Taylor who was also landlord of the Royal Oak and a few individuals with single fields. The Forestry Commission provided work for half a dozen villagers and one or two of us were employed further afield. Although farm machinery was being mechanised very rapidly most of the village farm work relied upon human and horse. The hay was cut with a horse drawn mower and turning and stacking was done by hand. There was great excitement when the Hickmans acquired an elevator, which made rick building a great deal easier. It seemed traditional for many villagers to assist in haymaking it was equally traditional for all concerned to assemble at the *Oak* at the end of the evening.

At the beginning of the century Hickman's farmhouse served a double purpose when it served as a post office. This was operated by the mother of the four brothers in an annex on the side of the farmhouse. From here a cable ran to a similar office in Cadnam over which telegrams could be sent. Each office had a dial with the letters of the alphabet and numbers one to ten around the perimeter; a pointer swivelled so that it could point to the required letter and the pressure of a switch recorded in the other office. Sending a message was obviously tedious and very slow but it was not greatly used. Most telegrams were for the tenant of Broomy Lodge, a sizeable house about three miles distant and Hedley usually had the job as delivery boy. Sometimes he delivered the message by bicycle, sometimes on horseback and sometimes on foot. If a family member took the message he usually received a six-penny tip, but if taken by the butler he departed empty handed!

For many years the postman delivered letters by bicycle, coming from Minstead Post Office. He came across country and his route along the bottom of North Bentley Inclosure is known as *Postman's Walk* to this day. During the first world war 1914 - 1918 news of the war's progress was scanty and it became routine for a precis of events to be pinned to the Post Office door so that villagers could come and read it. This was always done on a Sunday.

Hedley remembered vividly the day when the first aeroplane flew over Fritham. It was before the first world war and caused great excitement, he himself shinned up a tree so as to keep the machine in sight for as long as possible.

In the 1930's we had a good general store in the village on the left half way down the hill which leads to the Royal Oak. This had its own baker's oven and I well remember the baker, Jim Meech, with his long *paddle* pushing the dough into the glowing oven and the delightful smells that came from it. On the other side of the road further back up the hill was a bungalow, run by *Aunt Ivy* (as we called her) this functioned as a post office (long after Mrs Hickman's had closed) and she also sold sweets.

Looking back on these early days our village has not changed in any major respect; three or four new houses have replaced cottages which had fallen into disrepair and of course many dwellings have new occupants; but the traffic change is unbelievable; where once we could enjoy a quiet walk down an almost deserted lane to the *Oak* now it requires constant vigilance to avoid being run down by a speeding vehicle.

A very sad and major alteration to village itself was an incredible decision by the council to destroy the village pond, which had always been such a pleasant feature. The pond was situated on the green formed by the junction of Hydes lane and the road to the Royal Oak and I remember the moorhens used to nest in the bulrushes and other wild fowl used to pay frequent visits.

3. The pond at the bottom of Hydes Lane - opposite Whiteside Farm. A hayrick is on fire in the background. Moorhens, newts and dragonflies were just some of the wildlife found in and around the pond. Photograph taken by Cyril Batten 1920's

Shortly before his death ninety three year old Albert Bush, talking about his boyhood at the beginning of the twentieth century said "I never could understand why they filled in our pond: we village boys used to spend hours there watching the birds".

Perhaps in a more enlightened future the pond may be resuscitated and Fritham will rejoin the other villages which so value their ponds.

Fritham Memories by Janet Weir

In 1940 I came to Fritham. In 2000 I am still here. In 1940 I married again and therefore gave up looking after twenty-five landgirls in Lee-on-Solent. My new husband John said he had been posted to Gibraltar and we needed somewhere to live "so find somewhere". As I had loved the Forest since I was a child I went to Lyndhurst to, surprise, Hugh Pasmore's estate agency, and was given *To let, Moor Cottage Fritham.*

I took a bus (driver's name, Harrison - does anyone remember him?) He stopped everywhere for everyone, which made our journeys rather long. He stopped for me at the very beginning of Fritham Lodge and Fritham House. I stood for a moment or two breathing a quality of air unknown in Lee-on-Solent and said, "This is it. I never want to live anywhere else". Nor have I.

Moor Cottage looked over Stoney Cross and from its bedroom windows it seemed as though all the world's happenings could be seen. In 1942 the airfield was begun and the runways completed in 1943. All kinds of planes used it and from Moor Cottage I saw them all. One shattering day I watched a plane on fire come in and crash in a ball of flames. Nothing brought the war closer to those of us in Fritham who saw this tragic happening.

In 1956 Stoney Cross went back to the Forestry Commission and the runways were broken up, but to our extreme annoyance we were still prevented from driving across to Lyndhurst (a lovely little village in those days, not a tourist trap as it has become today).

By this time, 1947, we had moved with greatest regret from Moor Cottage to Whiteside Farm, a charming small house like a French farm house, with a walnut tree beside it, and an apple tree which had grown from a walking stick shoved into the ground, in front of it. I discovered later that the apples, borne abundantly on it were Morgan Sweets.

Mrs Soffe used to walk her pet cow up Hickman's lane and set it loose on the plain and then fetch it again at teatime when she also delivered the daily paper to me. One day she said, "When's the baby due?" I said. "What?" She repeated the question. I was flabbergasted and the next morning went to see Dr Sears and told him. He said, "There are lots of wise women like that. Let's see if she's right." And she was. Juliet was born in 1947. In those days there was no electricity and no mains water in Fritham. We had a spring under the flagstone kitchen floor. Granny Deacon who lived there before us used to lift the stone over the well and sweep the kitchen floor into it. I had looked down it and saw hand grips on either side. The men of the village told me that it was for smugglers to get down and hide their swag. There were quite a few smugglers here in days gone by. Perhaps there are some now, called by a different name?

I had the water tested of course by a man in the council offices. He said it was as pure as water could be. Thirty pumps filled the tank in the roof. We used my mother's beautiful brass oil lamps to light us, and after converting them to hold electrical lights we still do. Entertainment came from the wireless, cat's whiskers and glass valves, worked from big batteries, which had to be taken to Bramshaw garage to be charged. A far cry from very modern Fritham with digital television, surfing the net, the world-wide web and clicking with your mouse (CAN these expressions be right?).

Water and electricity came to Fritham at last. Even today that *at last* means just that. We are at the end of the line, and when there is a power cut these necessities are restored to us last of all!

Summers in Fritham by Margaret Houlgate

I spent my childhood summers in the 1920's with my grandparents at Valletta House in Fritham. As a young couple in 1879, Emily and Robert Bellamy had left their home in Bourne in Lincolnshire, and with their baby son Charles (my father), had taken up temporary residence in Mare and Foal cottage. Grandfather aged twenty-four was a Baptist preacher and had come to his first assignment, with the Schultze Gunpowder Factory. After about a year, the family moved into Valletta House, where my grandparents lived for the rest of their lives until 1930.

4. The Bellamy Family- 1883 Robert Bellamy aged 24, his wife Emily, son Charles and daughter Lily.

People in the village in those early days were mostly self-supporting with their own cows, hens and home grown vegetables, but produce was shared and excess milk put in great churns and left in the road to be collected early morning by a large cart drawn by two horses.

Granny's cool dairy had large flat dishes filled with milk. The cream was skimmed off for butter making in her churn, and the skimmed milk went to the noisy pigs. I can remember my grandmother sitting and turning the churn over and over, while my fingers itched to have a go, until at last I was allowed just a couple of heaves before being sent out to collect eggs or call the cows.

Wednesday was Ringwood market day, and the house was astir even earlier than usual, as my grandmother's famous butter, ready packed the night before, together with eggs and honey, was loaded into the pony and trap. My grandfather was a colporteur (a religious bookseller) and this was the day his bibles and religious tracts would be sold, so a pile of them was stacked on the floor of the trap with the butter.

On many glorious occasions I was allowed to accompany him on this long and exciting journey of thirteen miles across the Forest and into the seething activity of the market. I don't know how long it took Polly, the strawberry roan, to trot the distance but we took sandwiches and wedges of cake to sustain us, and I arrived back home tired but happy after what seemed to an eight year old, a long day.

When the hay was ready, I can remember the crop being cut with scythes, the men walking down the fields in line; as one field was finished the men all moved to another, and so all helped each other. When it was the turn of our fields, I took bread and cheese down to the workers, and together with the other children 'helped' rake up the hay, and then clambered up on to the laden cart for a ride up the hill or through the village. Bracken was also collected from the Forest, stacked and used for animal bedding.

5. Haymaking in the 1930's from left to right: Emily Soffe (nee Batten) with daughters Rose and May. Jack (John Batten), Gladys and Doris Batten. Alfred. Cyril Batten. Fred. 1931/2

As a child I roamed the Forest alone without fear. There were always forest workers about mending fences, digging ditches, clearing fallen trees, and all had a cheery word for me. Now the ditches are overgrown and trees lie where they fall - food for insects they say, but I think it is lack of willing labour, and the Forest has an unkempt and unloved look about it to my eyes. The ponies too have changed. Once they were small, brown with black manes and tails, and hardy. Now they come in all colours and are bred for riding.

In the 1920's there was no electricity or water in Granny's house, and every morning two buckets of water would be lifted from the well at the end of the garden, and carried back to the kitchen on a shoulder yoke. As a town girl I sometimes found it hard at first to share the same cold water in the enamel bowl, and had many a ticking off for throwing out the none too clean water when it was my turn to wash. My grandparents were both over seventy by then, and the buckets they had collected in the morning had to last the house all day. In the evening, there was the same weary trek to fill the water troughs for the animals. I can now well understand that I was not always flavour of the month!

I loved the daytime, but as the light faded and the farmhouse grew darker than anything the streets of Croydon could offer, I felt nervous. I wasn't keen on the candlelight, and could see shadows in all corners and clutching hands coming for me as I ran up the stairs to bed.

Much worse was the long cold and dark walk to the outside privy, where crickets and spiders shared the black, strong smelling brick house under the old walnut tree, and newspaper or old copies of Old Moores Almanac hung from a nail on the back of the door. Perhaps the first night I could persuade Granny to come with me, but after that I was on my own, and with a "Take a candle and be a brave girl" I would step out into the unknown. The candle flickered and sometimes went out leaving me in terrible blackness, and that is when I broke all Olympic records back to the welcoming light of the kitchen.

Most houses in those days did not enjoy the comfort we take for granted now. There was no central heating, no carpets and while the kitchen always had a fire with a black kettle on a hook, hissing quietly, the rest of house and bedrooms were cold and uninviting. My grandmother always wore a long black dress, and white apron, and I never saw her legs. Curtains were also dark, so that any rag rugs made from old dresses or curtains were very sombre.

But I can remember my bedroom with roses all over the wallpaper. Religious texts in their intricate wooden frames lined the walls, and in the corner stood a marble washstand with a rose decorated basin and ewer. I suspect my cold water morning 'wash' was more of a 'lick and a promise' and a weekly bath in front of the ever-burning kitchen fire took care of the corners I had missed. At night I would snuggle down in the large feather bed and look at the texts around me, especially the one that said "Be not afraid for I am always with you". I wasn't too sure about that one, and as I listened to the timbers creaking, on balance I felt I would be happier alone please!

Gypsies would come out of the Forest and walk through the village sometimes, and I loved to stand at the five barred gate and watch the piebald horses and the collection of dogs under the carts which rang with pots and pans hanging everywhere. The brown faced children and I would grin at each other, and I longed to run out and join them in their journey to the magical place they were bound for.

Fritham was a happy safe place in those days, with no cars and few visitors. I have such happy memories of days spent running in the forest, picking flowers, catching tadpoles, watching animals, 'helping' with the farm work and climbing trees with the local children. As an only child, I was happy to be alone sometimes, and at dusk I loved to go down to the gravel pits which had been dug out when the roads were put down to the factory years before. I would sit still as a mouse watching the many entrances to the rabbit warrens that peppered the bank. As darkness fell the rabbits would come out and start to feed, so that I was soon sitting, like Alice in Wonderland, surrounded by rabbits of all ages, seemingly unaware of my presence. It was magic. I hardly dared breathe. Surely the White Rabbit would appear at any minute, look at his watch and mutter "Oh my fur and whiskers!" Only Granny's "Coeeeee" from the distance would make me stir and I would realise how dark it had grown and it was time for tea back at Valletta. All this happiness didn't cost a penny.

Talking of which, my Grandmother gave me a penny a week pocket money, which was very generous in those days, and I spent a farthing at a time down in the dip in the village shop. I would rush down the hill and into the shop, the bell over the door announcing my arrival. I can still recall the smell of paraffin, soap, bread, animal feed, chocolate and goodness knows what else enveloping me. Mrs Bill Winter's heart must have sunk though, as spending my farthing was likely to take some time. I am sure I had more pleasure out of that weekly penny than many children today have with their money.

It would seem that religion was much more a part of village life in those days, and Fritham chapel was packed every Sunday for the morning and evening services, while my normally gentle grandfather spoke very sternly to what was obviously a naughty little village! Sitting in the back pew, I would stay very close to my grandmother, and with nervous glances at the open church door, hope the mysterious 'Wrath of God' would not arrive on that particular day.

These lovely days would end with the three of us sitting round the table as the oil lamp hissed quietly, granny would be mending while grand-dad wrote his next week's sermon. All too soon my Fritham holidays would be over, my father would come to take me home to Surrey, but before we left we would walk in the Forest, and he would show me places he had known and loved as a boy sixty years before.

He showed me the wild iris and gladioli, the rare orchids and ferns. He would point out the trout hiding in the forest streams and we would see the deer standing like statues until they caught our scent and ran silently, like phantoms through the trees. There was a wood where primroses were so thick on the ground it was impossible to walk without treading on them, and later the blue bells would make a sea of heady scented mauve blue. These treasures seem to have disappeared.

As well as the wild flowers, my father pointed out the Tortoiseshell, Red Admiral, Swallowtail, Purple Emperor and other butterflies, which fluttered in their dozens in inclosures. Now they have almost disappeared and a solitary coloured butterfly in the garden is cause for comment.

Compared to my bright sunny home in Surrey I can remember granny's house on the hill as rather dark, draughty and cold, but there was always laughter, bright fires, kittens and so much love and affection. Parishioners would call and leave a rabbit or brace of pheasants on the doorstep, as a thank you for butter or honey sent by my grandmother, and later I would again be sent running up to Mrs Somebody with some of granny's 'kill-or-cure' cough mixture. It was all go. My grandparents had very few worldly goods, and what they had they shared willingly. Looking back I now know they were very wealthy.

Memories of Fritham House by Elfrieda Fallowfield

Fritham House, with its arch and tower, stands guardian to the village of Fritham. Now it is known to us as a nursing home, but for me it was first and foremost my family home; becoming a temporary refuge for some exiled monks just after the war, before settling into its new role as a boarding school for girls.

Fritham House School was no ordinary school, as any ex-pupil (including one who has her home in Fritham Village) will testify.

There were not many other schools in the country, if any, where on Sunday evenings the pupils would gather in the book lined library, settle themselves down before the fire with their needlework, and listen enraptured to their headmaster, Sir Timothy Eden, reading aloud from books written by authors such as H. Rider Haggard, Charles Dickens, or the tear jerking Mrs Molesworth. As well as being read to they would also listen to classical music.

Where else would young girls learn to make in their needlework classes, not only the usual night-dresses, simple skirts and blouses, but also beautifully be-ribboned, lace trimmed exquisitely worked Christening dresses, for a day, way in their future lives, when they would be proudly used? My mother treasured the letters she received from old pupils who wrote to her long after they had left telling her THE dress had at last been used!

Pupils at Fritham House School were certainly given lessons in History, English Language, Literature, French, Mathematics and Science. These were deeply important subjects that were very well taught. Both my parents were fluent in other languages, and my mother was one of the first people to insist that conversational French should be taught from the earliest age possible. They both felt however, that more than just the usual academic subjects were needed to ensure a fully educated young woman graduated from their school.

Girls who were pupils at Fritham House learned how to read and understand silver hallmarks. They could look at a piece of furniture and tell if it was Chippendale or Hepplewhite. They could listen to a piece of music and know it if it was Mozart or Beethoven. They would study photographs of great buildings or monuments, and be able to tell in what country they could be found, or whether the columns were Doric or Corinthian. The works of famous artists held no mystery for them. They were encouraged to seek out, to discover, to explore, digest and discuss, but above all to appreciate beauty, not the least of which was to be found in the Forest in which their school was situated.

My father was a good amateur artist. His tree paintings are among his best. He painted in the studio, which was once, long ago, the village school. Many a pupil was whisked away from her playtime period to be forced, (often much against her will!) to 'sit for Sir Timothy'. Years later, after his death in 1963 these portraits were obtained by their sitters, most of whom were by then, married women. Their portraits were of great interest to their own children, and no doubt evoked many memories of their school days.

Great emphasis was place on literature. One of the pleasures of hearing Sir Timothy read poems, books and plays out loud was that he was able to act every part. For a short while in his younger days he had acted in the company of the famous actress Mrs Patrick Campbell.

This early experience, combined with a natural talent, made him a most gifted producer of plays. He had the ability to pick a child, often a seemingly unlikely one, and coax a performance out of her of almost professional standing.

I well remember on one occasion, all the parents were invited to watch a performance of 'Saul of Tarsus'. This was a play both written and produced by my father. A stage had been erected in the then garage, (now part of Fritham Court) and peeping through the curtain I saw the father of one of the girls sitting down for the performance with a look of utter boredom on his face. At the end of the play St. Paul lay dying. The girl who acted this part was quite brilliant. The bored father was surreptitiously wiping away tears from his eyes!

Music - all aspects of it - was very much part of school life. Girls from the school made up the choir for the services at St. Peter's in Bramshaw wearing rather extraordinary mauve choir robes and blue velvet berets. I remember many musical evenings in the drawing room singing, not only choral music, but ballads and old time music hall numbers to the accompaniment of the piano played either by my father or sister Rose.

Perhaps one of the reasons Fritham House was so unique was that it truly was a family school. Not only were both my parents very involved principals, but my sisters Rose and Amelia both worked in their time, either as extra teachers, or assisting the famous 'Clampie' (Mrs Clamp, the Matron) or helping wherever they were needed.

I, on the other hand was younger, and my early memories were not quite so happy! I hated my home being a school in term time. As I was studying ballet in London I only came to Fritham at the weekend. I used to find it very hard to discover there were parts of the house where I was not allowed to go. I resented being made to wear the uniform, being forced to 'obey the rules', having to eat in the school dining room and made to sleep in a dormitory, as my room was occupied. The older I grew the more I enjoyed it, as I could 'help'. No doubt this started my love affair with teaching which continues to this day.

The 'school' all waved goodbye to me when I left for an extended visit to New York. They were there again, agog with curiosity, when I returned with my future husband! Jane Twentyman (nee Sweet) was hand picked to play in a tennis game with us on one of the many grass courts laid out on the lawns.

Space does not permit me to wander unchecked down memory lane. Amelia, no doubt, would write from a very different viewpoint. Nor have I mentioned our eldest sister Ann, who valiantly took over the school after the death of my father, and debilitating stroke suffered by my mother.

With regret Ann decided the time had come to close the school which she had successfully continued to run for several years. For a while Fritham House reverted again to a family home, before it 'grew too big'. A more compact home was found, and Fritham House was sold. Over the ensuing years changes took place. The water tower; the engine house; the stables; garage and studio all were converted to individual homes. Finally, the main house became, as it is today, the New Forest Nursing Home.

Whiteside Farm by Janet Weir

Juliet aged about three or four had not been living at Whiteside for long before the County Council's children's officer asked me if I would look after a few babies.

I knew that I would love to do this and that I would be good at it. The garden was as near perfect as any garden could be, facing into the sun with a wide herbaceous border running down from the house to the road. *A few babies* would be happy in it.

In those days I used to turn to Lady Eden for advice. "Yes," she said "Ring them up and say yes, but no more than six!" Six! I had thought of two or three, but no "no more than six", she said. I should hope not. "And prams" said Lady Eden, the bit between her teeth "get them in Wimpole Street". Wimpole Street! I was going to advertise in the Echo. "Echo?" she said "second-hand prams! Certainly not, you wouldn't know who had been sleeping in them. I will order the right sort of prams for you." So she did and a few days later a van drove up and delivered six large beautiful sparkling prams. Cots came from Tyrells and soon the nursery was fully equipped. A stroke of luck, and looking back over the years I realise there were plenty of those. The newly retired matron of the Fenwick said she would like to come and be part of it, so in next to no time we were set up with a highly trained professional woman on our staff.

And then the babies came, five babies settling in each one according to his or her need, happy and contented. They were babies in need of knowledgeable and loving care, for a variety of reasons. We had twins whose mother was in prison. I wrote to the governor of Holloway, sending her a photograph of these beautiful little boys of about six weeks old, and asking why on earth arrangements couldn't be made for mother and babies to be together. She wrote back - no foster mother had to her knowledge tried to keep in touch. She was immensely grateful and the baby's mother was, of course, touched beyond belief. This has all been altered now, and in all womens' prisons there is nursery accommodation.

The arrival of the sixth baby was unforgettable. A London taxi drove up to the back door and out stepped a very handsome, beautifully dressed Nigerian woman. The beaming taxi driver reached into the cab and brought out a Moses basket with a lovely Nigerian baby in it. She was called Hannah. Her mother was a sister tutor at St Thomas' and her father a consultant. They both thought Hannah needed more constant attention than she got being fostered in London - but when her father's appointment was up she would go back to Africa with them as they set up a clinic there.

All the babies had one thing in common - the fresh air of Fritham, (this magical aura had the effect of making one mother not even recognise her baby after ten days with us).

Lady Eden used the nursery as a special treat for the girls at Fritham House School. They were sent down in twos and threes to look after the babies, wheel them about the garden, watch them being fed, and now and then shown how to bath them.

One day we piled all the babies into two local taxis and took them to Lyndhurst to be photographed by Yvonne Robertson. We practically brought

Lyndhurst to a standstill as one after the other we carried the babies into the studio. The photographs were superb - the best one was a long line of six babies with Juliet in the middle, and all so happy.

Even now this photograph is on show when we have a do in Fritham Free Church - and all kinds of people say, "Oh - do look - Mrs Wier's babies". Yvonne took one of Juliet holding Hannah, which caught the eye of a Methodist Minister. The very blonde child contrasted vividly with the very dark baby and I was asked if the Methodist church could use the photograph. Copies of it went around the world.

Thinking , remembering and writing about these babies has made me suddenly, with a jolt, realise that they would all now be almost fifty.

I wonder, heavens how I wonder, how they all are. Are they as well and as happy as they were in this lovely Fritham half a century ago? I must believe, and hope, and trust that they are.

Village Shopping by Margaret Pasmore

For a small village Fritham has boasted a number of shops over the years which were well patronised by the locals.

The most famous one was, surely, Mr. Winter's bakery and stores - this was well known not only for its delicious bread but also for doughcakes, lardy cakes, hot cross buns and the cakes made to order. The cover of an old order book announced 'Families waited on daily - cakes of all descriptions', - these were delivered to many houses around the area. But to go and shop there was an experience not to be missed. As you went down the steep little hill in the middle of the village, the aroma of freshly baked bread met you. Not only were there bread and cakes to buy but also groceries - sacks of sugar and flour which were ladled out and weighed on the scales. There were also brightly coloured sweets in tall jars. Mr Winter was very obliging - when the ovens were not in use at the weekend the villagers would bring to him the cakes they had mixed themselves and he would bake them - a very neighbourly thing to have done.

The Post Office, over the years, has been located in several different houses. The first one recorded was at New Farm, Hydes Lane where the postmistress was Mrs. Hickman senior. The next was opened in the White Cottage - a small wooden house in the middle of the village. It was run by Ivy Waters and had the Post Office at one end of the counter and the inevitable sweets at the other. It is said that you could also get your hair cut for the princely sum of three pence. The only telephone in the village was also there - in all a very useful shop.

Another fascinating shop was Primrose Cottage Shop close to Fritham

House - this was stocked by 'Bramshaw & District Co-operative Society Ltd.' run by Mrs Bush. This consisted of a corrugated iron shed on the side of the road by Primrose Cottage. It was very dark inside the shop and when you opened the door a bell rang to summon Mrs. Bush who would run out of the cottage to serve you. She sold a wide variety of goods, including black stockings and boots and haberdashery, etc.

6. Primrose Cottage Shop

In 1930 there was another sweetshop, opposite the Royal Oak, run by Mrs Bacon. Besides all these shops it was possible to buy eggs, vegetables, cream, milk and honey from the village farms and small-holdings.

In later years we became quite modern with a very comprehensive grocery and Post Office, managed most efficiently by Mr & Mrs Michael Stokes. This was situated in the middle of the village and was purpose built with living accommodation in the rear. It is now a private house called Brinton House.

Shopping in Fritham in those earlier years was a delight - lovely fresh food and the local gossip discussed freely - sadly there are now no shops in the village.

Account Shopping in Fritham by Elfrieda Fallowfield

I have the happiest memories of life in the village of Fritham when a small child. One of the highlights was walking with my mother to the Post Office (Mrs Walters) and then on down to the village shop - Winters.

What a perfect shop this was, with its large glass jars full of the most delicious and tempting looking sweets and bon-bons, and the huge slabs of butter, margarine and cheese behind the glass counter, all presided over by Mr Winter in his white overalls. My mother bought what was needed and if I was lucky - a few pear drops for me- and then said the magic words 'On account, please' - and left the shop, without paying a penny!

I was entranced at this brilliant way of shopping and decided to try it out for myself one day. In I went - bought my sweeties and said 'On account please' - it worked! Why doesn't everyone do that I wondered? It was so easy. Soon I gathered all my little friends in the village, and feeling very important took them in a little gaggle to the village shop. 'Have what you want,' I said, 'You don't have to pay'. I only have to say 'On account please'. The children were agog and did not need to be invited twice! Sweets, toffees, humbugs and peppermints galore were bought by happy war rationed children - I said the magic words - and we all trooped out of the shop.

My euphoria ended, however, by the time I arrived home. Mr Winter had thought to telephone my mother to explain what had happened. I was then give a stern lecture on the facts of life - namely that 'On Account' means 'Pay Later'.

A Cottage Story by Margaret Houlgate

When Valletta Cottage was being restored in 1972, the Architect examined the old hand made bricks, and believed that the long narrow single storey part of the cottage, was originally a cider house, used by the Royal Oak. He dated the bricks at over four hundred years old, but unfortunately it is difficult to prove any of this. Over the years, two small sitting rooms and two bedrooms were added and the *cider house* became the kitchen.

In the late 1800's the cottage belonged to Mr Briscoe Eyre, and his tenants at that time were Mr and Mrs Walter Winter. Walter had been the Coachman to Mr Griffiths at Eyeworth and he courted a London-bred housemaid, Cecilia who came with the Crosthwaithe-Eyre family from London to spend summers at Warrens. Full of high spirits, the family could not believe that this London girl would settle in the depth of the Forest, but settle happily she did. When Mr Griffiths no longer needed a coachman, Walter and Cecilia and their two sons moved into Valletta Cottage and worked the small holding until both were well in their nineties.

Around 1879, preacher Robert Bellamy and his family came from Lincolnshire, and took up residence in Valletta House, and at some time ownership of the house and cottage went from Briscoe Eyre to Robert and then to his son Charles Bellamy.

Cecilia (Daisy) and Walter continued to live happily in the cottage rent-free. Eventually my impoverished grandfather reluctantly had to ask for a little help with the repairs which were becoming increasingly necessary on the cottage and a rent of 2s 6d was agreed upon. This sum was still being paid in 1972 when Daisy died, and Robert Bellamy's grand-daughter Margaret came back to Fritham to live in the cottage.

To the end of her life Daisy refused to have water laid on, preferring to draw from the well every day. Electricity was completely vetoed, that new fangled gadgetry was never coming into her home. And the outside privy was much more hygienic than having a toilet inside. Whatever next! I worried about her. To my mind she was living in discomfort, but she would not let me make any improvements, or allow workmen into the cottage.

"Your grandfather promised me that I could stay here until I die," she said. "And it goes without saying that I will honour that promise" I readily assured her. But I did wonder whether the cottage would fall down in the next storm, or go up in smoke, as Daisy's method of cleaning the chimneys was to set fire to them!

I have a little notebook of Daisy's called *Visitor's Book* which records that during the years of 1907-1918 she had paying guests at Valletta Cottage, and their comments bring back memories of a world long gone.

June 14-21 1907

Mrs and Miss Tasker and Miss Moore have spent a delightful week with Mrs Walter Winter and have thoroughly appreciated her excellent cooking and punctuality. They feel the splendid air of Fritham has done them good.

October 15-27 1910

One can hardly imagine more excellent fare, more comfortable small rooms, more kindness and attention. All are provided by Mr and Mrs Walter Winter; combine them with a delightful neighbourhood and one cannot have a better receipt for health and happiness.

And in 1916 after a month's stay one visitor was really carried away with a two-page poem about Fritham scents, Fritham flowers, Fritham butter and Fritham cream "Everything Fritham is sure to please!"

It couldn't have been easy to entertain guests, without water, electricity and the amenities we take for granted. But Valletta Cottage was much appreciated by all who visited. It was a happy house - and still is.

Villagers Remember the 1920's, 1930's and 1940's

Maureen Bolton, Alfred Batten, Edwina Bright (nee Batten), Jeff and

Bernard Hickman, Bill and May Rogers, Gordon Thorne, Edie Winter and Fred Winter have provided the following memories:

Wages in Fritham

1934 - 7s a week for working from 6am- 4pm or 6pm at times

Before the war 10s a week as a lad working locally

Before the war £18 a year living in and working as a maid for Miss Henderson of Fritham Lodge. Every child in Fritham received sixpence from Miss Henderson at Christmas time. Miss Henderson herself distributed the sixpenny coins to the children on the school bus.

1942 - 16s a week

Entertainment

Villagers remember darts at the Royal Oak (but not on Sundays), socials in the Old School Room, used as a village hall during the war years. A mobile library in the form of a collection of books was stored in the Sunday School for villagers to use.

Childhood memories focus on playing in the Forest often from dawn to dusk. One villager can remember using an old door as a raft on Janesmoor Pond. Youngsters often cycled to Bramshaw to the dances.

Miss Stubbs of Woodlands, who was also the Sunday School teacher, organised a Happy Chums Club. The club met on weekday evenings to occupy the children with a range of games and activities. During the war years the club served a dual purpose of encouraging evacuees and village children to play together.

Village Entertainment in Pre-War Days

In the days prior to the Second World War villagers had few opportunities of enjoying entertainment in the village itself. After working hours buses were few and far between and private cars were only owned by the few more affluent villagers. The younger generation relied upon bicycles and the three Hickman brothers from New Farm recall that it was usual at weekends to cycle to Romsey, Salisbury and even Southampton to visit a cinema.

Fritham, however, had occasional local celebrations illustrated in a collection of notices and programmes:

Monday October 14th. 1895. At the Boys School Bramshaw in aid of the Fritham School. Doors open at 6.30 pm. Fritham Brass Band with fan dance by Miss Marjorie Eyre, song by Mr Eyre and tambourine dance by Miss D Eyre (others contributing were the Misses Thorne, Mr Dicker and Mr Davis).

Thursday May 11th. 1911. Fritham Band of Hope, Tea and Meeting at the Village Hall. (Band of Hope Prizes will be given to members for regular attendance and good conduct). Interesting miscellaneous programme including nail-driving and whistling competitions.

Tuesday March 13th 1928. At Fritham House Garage by kind permission of H.H.S. Northcote Esq., in aid of the Royal South Hants Hospital seventeen items comprising recitations, songs, sketches and community singing (over 40 villagers named).

May 6th 1935 H.M.King George's Silver Jubilee Celebration at Fritham House Garage at 2pm. Races and competitions. Children's and Adult's teas. Prizes will be presented by Mrs Holroyd.

May 12th 1937 King George VI and Queen Elizabeth's Coronation. 13 Fancy Dress and Race competitions. Prizes presented by Lady Eden.

June 2nd 1953 Fritham Coronation Celebrations 11.30am. Children's sports followed by adults' sports. Children's tea, adult's buffet. Planting and dedication of Coronation tree. Social evening in Fritham House Garage, followed by dancing and games. 12.00pm Bonfire. By kind permission of Sir Timothy and Lady Eden.

Auction at the Royal Oak

In 1962 a former villager of Fritham remembers Ivy Lea and Dovecote coming under the auctioneer's hammer in the back room of the Royal Oak. He purchased Dovecote for £350.

Water in Fritham by Alf Batten and Edwin Bright (nee Batten)

In the 1920's a number of children collected the water for their respective families from the springs in a large 44 gallon wooden barrel. The barrel was on a swivel axle to allow for movement and prevent spillage. It was a cart construction with iron handles and supports with rubber over the handles.

The carrier was given by the Gunpowder Factory to nearby villagers around the Free Church (Chapel) and kept covered up under the oak tree opposite ready for use. Children usually did this task as the photograph portrays. The carrier was previously in constant use at Eyeworth by the cottagers who lived in the Powder Mill cottages complex. The water for their use was collected from a constantly running pipe out of the hillside on the right hand side of reservoir. Surplus was collected in an iron tank let into the ground beneath the running pipe. Excess from the tank ran beneath the man-made gravel road and into the reservoir. The reservoir was never called Eyeworth Pond in past years as it was man-made purposely for the use of the Powder Mill factory. The gravel road beside the reservoir and the stream which supplied the water was always kept well cleaned out and the irons well also. The reservoir used to be regularly drained and cleared of withy, reeds, weeds, etc., and the steps and valves inside the iron railings kept in working order. The large iron pipe, that took the water from the reservoir, can still be seen going beneath the road to the factory.

7. The Water Carriers: from left to right, Maurice and Stan Winter, Lily and Doris Batten, Alf and Cyril Batten, The Moody Brothers

A piped water supply came into the village around 1951 allowing many adults and children to dispense with the above routine of drawing water and delivering it to other villagers. One villager remembers having three buckets of water every day to cover all washing and cooking. Rainwater was also collected to provide a further supply for hair washing and general washing complete with midges. At times water for cattle was collected in old milk churns.

Fritham Cricket by Hugh Pasmore

Little is known of the history of the village eleven. It is recorded in the excellent history of the Bramshaw Cricket Club that Fritham United was playing as early as 1859 and again in the early 1900's. Nothing further is known until shortly before the second world war in 1939. At that time one of the McAlpine family was renting the furnished Fritham House from Mrs Holroyd and he generously provided a thatched cricket pavilion placed in front of The Butt indicating the team was well established. During the war the 7 ft. high fence around the airfield embraced the whole of the cricket pitch and the pavilion was dismantled. It was not until about 1947 that the airfield fencing was demolished and the village cricket team re-established. The problem was that such a small village found difficulty in fielding eleven players, the more especially when hay-making was in progress and outside help was often called upon to supplement actual villagers. There were no restrictions as to garb, and as not everyone possessed white flannels a variety of unorthodox clothing appeared on occasion.

In view of the disappearance of the pre-war pavilion Norman Winter's old lorry was substituted and this served as a cover for the refreshments. An essential part of these was a cask of ale or cider which was much appreciated by both teams.

At the time my wife and I lived in the White House which lay at the end of the lane overlooking the cricket pitch as well as the Hickman Brothers' milking shed on one side and their dairy on the other side of the road. Each brother in turn as he filled his bucket took it across the lane for cooling in the dairy and inevitably, as each reached a point at which the pitch was visible, downed his bucket on the road and watched a couple of bowls and a possible run!

8. The Fritham Cricket Team

A former villager, Charles Sillence, remembers some aspects of the cricket matches very well:

' We did not arrive at Fritham until the mid fifties when there was no team as such. The games we played in the late 50's and 60's were from the Royal

Oak darts team at that time and the venue was the old airfield wherever we found a level strip of grass. We used Norman Winter's horse trailer as a pavilion and the Colonel provided the cider (strongest we could muster). The aim was to get the opposing team to consume as much as possible before sending them in to bat (not quite cricket really but it worked). I can remember Dr. Eldon being one of the umpires and Alistair Holloway and George Lye being the bowlers and Fred Winter taking the furthest outfield nearest the woods in case of bladder pressure! There was no pretence of serious cricket and the audience joined in the celebrations. Major Bleasby was wicket keeper, complete with pith helmet salvaged from his army days - we won't see those days again.'

CHAPTER FOUR

Fritham at War

For a small country village Fritham had an unusually large involvement in the Second World War. The construction of an aerodrome was obviously its principal involvement, followed by the gradual exodus of villagers to join the various branches of the services (refer to appendix 1 for further details). Fritham's final contribution was the formation of its own fighting force in the way of its Home Guard unit. Immediately after Great Britain had declared itself at war with Germany in 1939 the Foreign Secretary, Anthony Eden, announced on the radio that throughout the country volunteers were urgently required to form local defence units to combat enemy forces which might make surprise attacks by landing on the beaches or parachuting from the air.

Villagers throughout the country immediately set about recruiting their own groups willing to defend their area. Gerald Forward, a leading villager who had seen service in the First World War, immediately volunteered his services, and was officially appointed the head of the Fritham unit.

9. Gerald Forward, Agister and Head of Fritham's Home Guard Unit

Gerald was an Agister, appointed by the New Forest Court of Verderers to supervise the animals depastured on the open Forest and of course knew the northern part of the Forest intimately so was an obvious choice as leader of the unit.

In addition to the Fritham villagers who quickly volunteered to enlist, Gerald was able to call upon a team of 60 lumberjacks from Newfoundland who were employed by the Forestry Commission and were living in log cabins they had built in the woodland north of the Village.

Home guard units were, of course, attached to the British army and were subject to army discipline and individuals went on courses on explosives, etc. Each man was issued with an army 300 rifle with ten rounds of ammunition. The only time, apart from target practise, that a bullet was fired was one night when Southampton was being heavily bombed with the occasional bomb falling on the Forest. On this occasion one of the lumberjacks saw a light showing in Fritham House and promptly put a bullet through the window. He explained afterwards that in view of the fierce air raid over Southampton he thought a spy might have been signalling the bombers!

Later in the war a Regular Army staff officer visited the Unit and told Gerald that there was a scheme whereby if the enemy succeeded in invading this country, small units would go under cover and operate to harass the enemy behind the lines. Fritham elected to join the project and forthwith hideouts were constructed in various places in the more remote woodland. One of these hideouts involved a small caravan which came from the Warrens estate (with the approval of John Crosthwaite-Eyre). This was towed by car and tractor to a remote spot and completely buried. Fortunately the invasion never materialised and the caravan was disinterred after the war.

All that now remains of the Fritham Home Guard is a studio photograph of the 16 villagers in their khaki uniforms, none of whom is still alive.

10. 1945 9th. Hants (Forest) Battalion, Home Guard. Comprising Fritham Villagers
Back row: Hedley Hickman, Mick Rogers, Reg. H., Arthur H., Ted Hickman.
Middle row: Jim Soffe, Vic Winter, Bill Quinton, Bert Williams, George Millard, Alf Parnell, Geo. Munden.
Front row: ? Dr. Pesel, Saunders, Fred Carter, Albert Bush.

Stoney Cross Airfield 1942 - 1947

The airfield at Stoney Cross has a well-documented history during this period. What follows is an account of that history taken from the memories of past and present villagers of Fritham.

Villagers who lived at the top of Hydes Lane remember work commencing at Stoney Cross in 1942. This project was to be the last of the New Forest's three airfields. In the first year 442 acres were appropriated to the airfield with an additional 70 acres in the following year. Originally Stoney Cross was to be a secret airfield, surrounded by the wooded enclosures, which offered natural camouflage for the aircraft. Construction of the airfield by Wimpeys and local sub-contractors took eighteen months, due to a shortage of appropriate materials and labour.

A high wire fence was built around the perimeter to exclude both animals and humans. Compensation of £2 per head per annum was paid to local farmers for loss of grazing for their cattle. The airfield stretched from Ocknell Pond up to the A31 along the A31 to Ocknell Firs at Stoney Cross, as far as the Compton Arms and down to the bottom of Longbeech and then along the outside of Kings Garn to Hickman's Green (The Butts). The Officers' and Sergeants' messes, the Church and the gymnasium were all situated in Longbeech Wood, whilst aircrews occupied the Ocknell site stretching round Winding Stonard with the bomb dump in Anses Wood close to the subsequently built Cadmans Pool.

The building of the airfield created a number of problems for some of the villagers. At one time the officials decided that Moor Cottage and New Farm would be demolished but fortunately for the occupants this threat did not materialise. One villager has memories of her father striding round the family home in Fritham House, muttering and cursing under his breath as the Ministry decreed that many of the trees in the garden must be cut down as they were in direct line with the intended flight path. Mature oaks and beeches in North Bentley Inclosure were felled together with a line of trees in front of Fritham Cottage. An alternative water trough on Hickman's Green was provided to replace Janesmoor Pond, which came within the confines of the airfield. A German governess and the butler of Fritham House were marched off to an internment camp when they were found to be making maps of the construction of the aerodrome during a daily bicycle ride. Many of the villagers had to find an alternative route to Lyndhurst as they were no longer permitted to travel across Stoney Cross. However, Hedley and Evelyn Hickman who lived at the top of Hydes Lane were granted permits to cross the airfield as was Albert Bush in order to cycle to his work at the West Hants Electricity Company based in Lyndhurst.

The children in the village were drawn to the airfield and many have vivid memories of their escapades. They would slip through the fence, run up the canvas that formed the back of the hanger and slide down. At other times the children would climb on the planes and on one occasion an open door provided the opportunity to explore and pull the ripcord of a parachute which billowed around them. This experience frightened them sufficiently to delay a return visit for some time. It was not unknown for the children to gain access to one of the telephones in the airfield huts and to use the displayed telephone list to ring up different numbers such as 'grocery stores' and 'dentist'. However, 'RAF officers' who giggled when ordering ice cream to be delivered to the hut were soon uncovered. After a few of these calls, a jeep would arrive to investigate and the children would dash madly, hearts pounding, into the Forest and safety. The children made good use of the discarded fuel tanks that were jettisoned on landing. These torpedo-shaped tanks were cut in half and used as canoes on Dockens Water.

11. Doreen, Dorothy and Jean Soffe at the old disused Guard Room of Stoney Cross Airfield circa 1950

Gliders were towed up to practise making circles and parachutes were dropped over Slufters. Throughout the second half of 1943 there was intense activity at Stoney Cross as forces were built up in preparation for the invasion of Northern France. On one part of Stoney Cross an American unit was set up to assemble American built Waco CG4 A Gliders that had been shipped across the Atlantic in sections, five crates per glider. After assembly the gliders were towed away to American bases in Southern England. One windy night a newly constructed glider was blown over the fence and smashed.

In 1944 when the invasion was imminent the operational crews were transferred to Brize Norton and the role of Stoney Cross was changed. The Americans moved in with Lightnings and Mustangs and for some months they used the base for fighting over France. The Americans 'personalised' their aircraft with names such as 'Kozy Koza', 'Little Buckaroo', and 'Lucky Irish'. The drawings illustrating these names on the side of the aircraft were wonderfully vivid. The Lightnings usually had their engines started up at 3 a.m. but villagers living at the top of Hydes Lane became so used to the noise they hardly noticed. Time and again villagers who were children then remember the planes coming back with holes in the fuselage. Crashes also occurred within the airfield itself and the surrounding area. Villagers remember the pilot who crashed in North Bentley and broke his ankle as he slid down a tree to safety. One night two villagers, Evelyn and Hedley Hickman, were walking past Janesmoor House on the way to their fields when two Lightnings came in to land on the North South runway. Just before touch down a red flare was fired in front of them, presumably indicating some obstruction and both machines swept upwards almost vertically, then one swerved dramatically and dived straight into the ground on the petrol road opposite Janesmoor House, bursting into flames.

The Americans found the accommodation at Stoney Cross far better than the tented camps so many other U.S. units were provided with. Denis Bush remembers how the Americans allowed him and his cousin to sit in the cockpit of the plane. The Americans would collect the children of Fritham in their lorries and entertain them for tea and a film show in the huts near the Control Tower at Long Beech.

The most poignant memory of all must be the child who remembered the army lorries arriving just before D-Day. Lines and lines of trucks brought airborne troops to Stoney Cross Airfield. The troops were camped overnight in North and South Bentley inclosures before continuing their journey to Southampton Docks for embarkation. A number of the soldiers had brought a book or a Bible that had to remain behind when they departed. In some cases the books were just left in the open while others had tried to hide or bury their books and belongings.

On 15th September 1945 the airfield held its RAF Open Day under the last Commanding Officer of Stoney Cross, Group Captain C.C.O' Grady. The demonstrations emphasised the Overseas Passenger work of the airfield but there were also visiting aircraft from other RAF stations to add interest.

Local councils later used the living areas within the camp as temporary housing for families. Some of the hangars were taken over by the Home Office to store 'Green Goddesses' (fire engines) and motor cycles that had been withdrawn from Civil Defence use. Another hangar was used to store surplus supplies such as grain and bales of rubber. When the war ended the airfield remained enclosed with locked gates, much to the annoyance of the villagers who needed to get to Lyndhurst daily. This was at a time when petrol was on coupons and precious. In 1946 a number of villagers started a campaign of cutting the chains and padlocks under cover of darkness. In 1947 the airfield was finally opened for access.

The 367th. Fighter Group USAFF arrives at Stoney Cross
by Alan Brown (Minstead)

On the 3rd. April 1944 the men of the 367th. Fighter Group arrived by ship at Greenock in Scotland and took the train south to their first base in Europe at Stoney Cross. After a long and tiring overnight journey they arrived by truck at the airfield. It had been used by RAF squadrons of glider towing and paratrooping aircraft. It would be an ideal fighter base, but the pilots' spirits sank as they saw eighty-five P38 Lightning, twin engined fighters parked around the airfield for their use. Only four of the hundred pilots had flown a P38 before and all the others had been trained to fly only single engined fighters and had hoped to be flying the much vaunted P51 Mustang.

Captain Jimmy Peck DFC an American pilot who had flown with the RAF in defence of Malta, quipped, 'Well that is about the last straw'. However, he was one of the first to try. A week later the rest of the pilots watched in horror as Jimmy Peck was killed in front of them trying to land a P38 with one failed engine on his first Stoney Cross flight. Despite their fears there were no other types for the pilots to fly and the group had to learn to fly them and be ready for their first operations over France in early May. There were several crashes in training without the loss of lives and by the 9th. of May Colonel Young led forty aircraft over France. From then on the pilots began to appreciate their twin engined fighters more and more for flights over enemy territory.

Meanwhile the men had settled in at Stoney Cross. At least they had clusters of Nissen huts to live in whereas most other 9th. Air Force groups moving into the Forest Advanced Landing Grounds had to make do with tented accommodation. At Stoney Cross it was fourteen to a hut with a small metal stove for heating. Sgt. Ernie Snow described it as a useless device that defied all attempts to get it hot. American groups arriving in Southern England straight from the USA in 1944 were of the opinion that they were right in the combat zone and prepared for anything. Ernie describes the elaborate plans in case a German paratroop landing attempted to capture their huts. Frequent air raid alerts frightened the men at first and they dived into slit trenches, but they soon became accustomed to the wailing sound and stood on vantage points to watch raids on Southampton from a distance. They soon realised that work went on in Britain even during an alert unless they were under direct attack.

The men of the group settled down to working long hours in the build up to D Day. On the 6th. of June the Lightning fighters with their distinctive shape were used for low support of the landings as they were less likely to be mistaken for enemy aircraft. On the 22nd of June after sixteen days of round the clock support of the troops ashore, the aircraft of the 367th joined an attack on Cherbourg and suffered heavy losses and damage. Seven pilots were killed and only thirteen out of the forty-eight planes employed could be used again that day. Ernie Snow said the pilots were shaken by their experiences and landed their damaged aircraft all over the airfield. The next day the group had to be stood down from operations, but ground crews worked all day and night to have aircraft ready to continue attacks on the 24th and so the attacks went on until the group moved to Ibsley on the 5th. of July.

(Readers may wish to consult Alan Brown's book please refer to the bibliography)

Life at Stoney Cross by Roy Jackman (Lyndhurst)

I was demobilised from the RAF in April 1946 and in May I married Eileen. We went to live at Pikes Hill, Lyndhurst. Eileen heard that the District Council was allowing people to live in the huts at Long Beech, Stoney Cross. So one Saturday we put Stephen, who had just been born into the pram and walked to Stoney Cross. We had no car then.

In September 1947 we moved into Hut 336, Long Beech, Stoney Cross. The old aerodrome was not in use and the New Forest Rural District Council, as it was then, took over the huts for housing. This housing was for people coming back from the War. We stayed there until July 1950.

There were about three hundred families on the site. Most were in Nissen huts, though some had Officer's quarters. The Nissen huts were made of corrugated iron, but the Council had divided them in half and then half again, giving a living room and two bedrooms. Water and electricity were already installed. The Council put in electricity meters and a coal fire cooking stove. The rent was five shillings a week.

The community soon got organised, and formed a committee. They got in touch with the Hants and Dorset Bus Company and had a bus from the Water Tower (Stoney Cross) to Southampton. The Skylark Motor Services of Redlynch provided a bus to Salisbury.

There was a good gymnasium where we had dances, children's parties and other social events, including a cinema. At the end of the gymnasium was the Camp Chapel. This was used by the Church of England; the Roman Catholics and a non-conformist Elim Four Square Gospel Church. Father Blake came out from Lyndhurst for the Catholics until Lady Eden's Fritham House was taken over by a school of young men training for the priesthood. We went there for services and picked mushrooms for breakfast on the way home.

We had a little shop and a resident nurse. The doctor came once a week. A van came round with fish, milk, groceries, vegetables and coal. A fish and chip van stopped near the Water Tower (Stoney Cross). Some people kept chickens and sold the eggs. The ground was too hard and poor to grow vegetables. There was plenty of wood about. If you wanted a pint, it was a short walk through the woods to the Sir Walter Tyrell.

The WAAF site was later used by the gypsies when the Forestry Commission closed the Shave Green site. The gypsies only used the huts for sleeping in, doing their cooking outside as they had always done.

Thoughts of an Evacuee by Evelyn Amos (nee Blackie, Hythe)

Evelyn Amos (nee Blackie) became a 'temporary' villager during the war years. Her account of how she came to Fritham is quite remarkable:

'Although it is almost sixty years since I first became an evacuee some memories are still vivid. Waiting to board a charabanc outside Southampton's Guildhall on Saturday 2nd. September 1939 with my nametag, gas mask and tiny bag of belongings, I remember feeling very confused. We were transported to Bournemouth leaving behind tearful mothers. On arrival we were allocated or chosen by our foster parents and I was lucky to be billeted with a very kind lady who had two children of her own and then two more evacuees. I was reasonably happy but naturally missed my mother.

When the bombing began, Southampton was a major target but Bournemouth didn't escape entirely and when a stray bomb fell just a little way from my billet mum decided I should go back home. Then came the blitz in November 1940, we spent every night in air raid shelters and emerged each morning to view the devastation. On one particular occasion we were amazed to see that all the shops on the opposite side of our road had been hit and the smell of burning rubber from Mr. Pope's bicycle shop is still a powerful memory. The following night we went to my Gran's house in another area of the town, once again the siren sent us to the shelter, we heard a tremendous explosion and Gran was certain her house had been hit, when the 'all clear' sounded we all came out of the shelter to discover the house next door had been razed to the ground. A wrought-iron gate from the house opposite had been blasted through Gran's bay window. There was glass everywhere and to add insult to injury every cup and saucer on the dresser had been shattered. It was this last incident that made mum decide to seek a safer place for us to stay. Subsequently we set off for Fritham.

Our trek to the village is a happy memory. I do remember crossing the Totton Causeway on foot and my mother knocking on doors as we made our way through the village. Reaching Fritham Farm we saw the friendly face of Mrs Quinton peering over the garden gate. I'll never forget the relief when that dear lady said 'You'll do'. She took us in and introduced us to the family, Mr Quinton (who became Uncle Bill), the farmer and Valerie their only daughter.

It was agreed that Mum would work on the farm in return for our accommodation and food. She learned to milk cows, muck out and anything that was required. For me it was an idyllic time. Of course initially I was terrified of those huge cows and the cart horses Punch and Ginger and even the cockerels. However, helping to collect eggs and feeding the pigs soon became part of daily life. Highlights were when the combine harvester arrived and everyone helped each other. Mrs Quinton (or Auntie Edie as I now called her) would make huge enamel jugs of tea and there would be bread and jam and home-made cakes for all to share.

The huge barn was used to store winter bedding and made a great playground too, it also housed a contraption like a giant mincer which chopped the mangels into big chips and also fed the animals, sometimes I ate some. In spring searching for the first primroses was another joy and each field on the farm had a name - 'the paddock', 'the meadow', and 'eight acres' - the best primroses were in the latter.

Sunday meant a trip to Sunday School at the little chapel and quite often a long walk into Brook across the Forest ending with a drink at The Green Dragon and then the long trek home.

The arrival of the Americans at Stoney Cross Aerodrome caused great excitement (and consternation for some). These young men so far from home needed friendship and contact with families. Three lads in particular became regular visitors to the farm and were thrilled to barter such luxuries as canned peaches for fresh eggs. We called them the three musketeers for they seemed inseparable. Sadly after one night mission in their Lockheed Lightning planes only one flier came back. The two younger boys had been shot down presumed dead and John had to break the news to us. It was like losing members of our own family.

I was lucky to find many friends in the village and remember being allowed to help Rosemary Gee to pick beautiful big golden gooseberries in the gardens of Fritham House. Rosemary's Dad was the gardener. Here also I was quite overawed at the sight of some young ladies on horseback in full riding gear. They were related to Sir Timothy Eden I believe, and they looked splendid and spoke so beautifully.

Lastly school days were very happy. At Bramshaw I received a good start and lots of encouragement when it came time to sit for my scholarship. The school dinners were excellent considering all the wartime shortages; an especial favourite was the chocolate pudding and custard. On one occasion I recall we were unable to go to school because of deep snow. Our school bus had been stuck on Piper's Wait Hill near Nomansland! When the result of my scholarship came and I had passed we had to decide which grammar school I would attend. St Anne's was my first choice but it did mean being evacuated yet again to Bournemouth. So in September 1944 I left Fritham Farm for pastures new. However the Quintons were forever our friends and we visited them whenever possible.'

Fritham Village during the War Years

The other parts of the village at Eyeworth and Fritham Plain were also involved in the war effort. A gunsite for targeting enemy planes was located near Green Pond and a searchlight was positioned just before Eyeworth Lodge on the left hand side.

During the war years Canadian lumberjacks built log cabins for army personnel at Fritham Springs near Green Pond. The wood was provided from the Forest and the cracks were sealed with moss. Italian prisoners of war also worked within this area. Maurice Winter supervised these prisoners of war on their way to work at the Saw Mills in Sloden. Denis Bush remembers accompanying his father, who was in the Home Guard, to firing practice in a pit on the Amberwood Road. Amberwood was used as a bombing range during the war.

There appear to be few accounts of bombs actually hitting targets in Fritham apart from a bomb that was dropped in front of Homefield that damaged the house and the Chapel. All the front windows of Homefield were shattered as well as the Chapel windows facing this area. The ceiling in the older part of Homefield dating back to 1682 fell in. Present day cracks in the wall of the Chapel provide a reminder of that incident. However, Fritham was still regarded as safer than many other areas with some villagers storing valuables such as Turkish carpets and other items of value for friends who lived in Southampton.

Moving down the hill Norman Winter's shop also featured during the war years. Norman Winter, Mr Williams and one other always baked and delivered the bread and cakes, including a particularly good lardy cake. The bakers had special bags for putting lardy cakes in. On this occasion the baker had put the bags in the bread mixer for safe keeping overnight. The next morning the bread mix was put into the mixer and the machine switched on. The interesting bread mix with pieces of shredded paper had to be disposed of discreetly. A villager remembers the set of swill bins kept at the back door of the bakery. The said mixture was put into these swill bins but the top of the swill bins kept rising as the yeast fermented! What a feast for the appreciative pigs!

V.E. day celebrations took place in the courtyard of Fritham House by kind permission of Sir Timothy Eden.

Wartime Ice Storms

In January 1940 Fritham was five months into the Second World War. The weather during January had been very cold with temperatures falling to -6F (-21C). Towards the end of the month on the 26th of January a snowstorm brought much of the nation to a standstill. At this time Fritham suffered an amazing weather phenomenon - an ice storm.

12. Ponies being fed hay in severe weather conditions

The ice storm was the result of supercooled raindrops falling into the air near the ground that had a temperature well below freezing. As the raindrops fell they froze as soon as they came in contact with any object they hit. This created an amazing effect. Ice built up on houses especially those with eastern and southern aspects resulting in doors and windows freezing shut. Trees became encased in ice and the boughs broke under the weight. Often the sound of this ice cracking would be similar to gunfire - not a desirable sound considering the nation was at war. In the shrubs and hedges of Fritham the leaves became iced and rattled noisily as the breeze blew through them. Animal life also suffered.

During this ice storm Fritham was cut off from the outside world for 48 hours. Roads became impassable and all the telephone wires were brought down. The children who normally went to school in Bramshaw by bus enjoyed an unexpected holiday. There had been no newspapers in the village for a number of days. A postal delivery resumed after the sub-postmaster at Minstead, Mr Howells, and his daughter had trudged along the long straight road over the highest parts of the Forest, carrying the mail in sacks and frequently falling into the deep drifts and hidden ditches. When they arrived late in the evening the sub-postmaster at Fritham, Mr. P. Walters and Mrs. Walters completed the delivery on foot which involved making their way through snow a foot deep to reach the farms and cottages of Fritham.

13 A photograph of the first postal delivery during the ice storm (Echo Newspaper)

Mr Winter the village baker made four attempts to drive his van up the road and through the village and eventually had to give up. The only vehicle that managed to get through during these conditions was a brewery lorry bringing much needed refreshment to the Royal Oak.

One poor motorist finding himself marooned on the road at Minstead staggered to Fritham House, where Sir Timothy Eden, gave him hospitality for the night. Two maidservants at Fritham House tried to walk from Bramshaw one night but had to obtain shelter at Brook. They arrived at Fritham the following afternoon exhausted after struggling through snow that was almost waist high. However, the winter sports enthusiasts enjoyed splendid skiing conditions on the long slopes of Fritham.

CHAPTER FIVE

Fritham Buildings of Interest

Fritham Free Church by Margaret Houlgate

A church, a school, a pub and a shop - every village is expected to have one and Fritham 166 years ago was no exception.

In 1833 there was a Particular Baptist Chapel at the far end of the village near the green. It had a membership of 60, with a morning attendance of 30 and an afternoon group of 40, and John James, the minister travelled from the village of Downton to take the services.

The Baptists are a Christian denomination founded in Holland in 1609 by John Smyth, a clergyman who had broken away from the Church of England. He was convinced that only adult believers should be baptised by immersion, and was therefore against infant baptism.

There were two branches of Baptists, the Particular Baptists (following the theology of John Calvin), who held that only a minority, the elect, could gain salvation and were predestined to do so, and the General Baptists who held that the gospel should be preached to all.

Thus in 1833 it would appear that Particular Baptists practised in Fritham Chapel, but over the next few years there was a joining with the General branch, and the services became more liberal.

The Chapel had had a chequered history with times of plenty, followed by closure when interested parties died. A new building and school was built in 1861, and was opened officially in 1862 by the Bishop, a ceremony followed by "a lunch and garden party". But did the attendance falter yet again after a while? Records show that 13 years later, in 1874, the chapel was re-opened by Mr Griffiths, the manager of the Schultze Gunpowder Factory.

1904 saw a great change in the Chapel, when on 12th January it became Fritham Free Church United, welcoming preachers from all denominations, and a new brick building was proposed. This was to be built by Schultze under the direction of Mr Griffiths, who was a keen supporter of the church, and was to take the place of the original green painted corrugated chapel, known by some as "The Hut".

The new brick building was welcomed by the villagers, and the Fritham Free Church Building Fund was set up in February 1904. During a busy year of fundraising, donations were given by every member of the community with sums ranging from 5 shillings to £100 (from Mr Griffiths) and the fund closed with a sum of £970. 2s 7d, a mighty communal effort in 1904 when the average rural wage was fifteen shillings. Unfortunately Mr Griffiths died whilst on holiday in Egypt and the church lost a great supporter and Fritham mourned a good friend.

Under the dedicated and enthusiastic care of preacher Robert Bellamy, the church flourished and in 1906, it was bought for £50 by the Trustees for them and their successors. If sold in the future, the money was to go to any Protestant Church.

The tin chapel was the scene of much activity with concerts, meetings, ladies sewing circle, and teas, and a bill from Mr W E Winter's grocer shop for 60 lb. cake, 6 gallons of bread, 4 lb. tea, 10 lb. lump of sugar, 7 lb. butter and two and a half gallons of milk came to £2. 9s. 9d. The brick church was heated by coal (£1.6s 6d a ton) a boiler in an outside shed had to be stoked up for the winter services, and huge pipes ran around the church. In the 2000's these pipes are redundant, and the church is warmed by electricity with a flick of a switch.

On May 11th 1911 there was a public tea and annual meeting of the Band of Hope, when prizes were given to Members for regular attendance and good conduct, and this was followed by a nail driving competition and a whistling contest.

The Band of Hope, with its messages of temperance was very strong in Fritham, and a little poem, written on an old concert programme, in childish handwriting with crossings out, recently discovered in the archives was obviously this 8 year old's recitation for the occasion.

The Three Little Boys
The second little boy spoke to the first little boy
As the first little boy stood by
The third little boy saw the first little boy
Look down on the ground and cry

So the third little boy asked the first little boy
What the second little boy had said
The first little boy eyed the third little boy
And blushed and hung his head

The second little boy pressed the first little boy
To answer his question quick
So the first little boy told the second little boy
That his daddy was Drunken Dick.

Then the second little boy and the third little boy

Tried the first little boy to cheer
And the third little boy got the first little boy
To sign against wine and beer

Then the first little boy told the second little boy
(I think that was good don't you)
That since he had signed the Temperance Pledge
His daddy had signed it too

In the pre radio and television days, between the wars, one very popular activity which took place in the old chapel was the Sunday School, attended by most of the children in the village, under the care of Miss Stubbs, who also ran a Happy Chums Club for them in her cottage 'Woodlands'.

14. Fritham Sunday School circa 1910

Another good friend who regularly came from Eastleigh to help with the School and church was the Rev. Dainton. I wonder how he dealt with the sow and her piglets which were 'accidentally' shut in the hut by one of his youthful congregation one Sunday!

The church served the community during the first and second world wars, and in fact, suffered broken windows and structural damage when a bomb dropped a few hundred yards away. Gerald and Alice Forward held weekly whist drives in their home, making a small charge for the evening. When they had accumulated £50 this was offered to the Trustees for the restoration of the hut, which had fallen into disrepair several years before, so that it could be used for social activities. The Trustees decided they could not accept the money which had been involved with gambling, and the offer was not accepted! The old building was eventually taken down about 1960.

The photograph of 'Free Church, Fritham' depicts the old building and the goats that always wandered around the church area. The goats slept beneath the stage end of the small old tin church in the graveyard area.

15. Fritham Church with the goats

Sadly, once again, numbers dropped and the new brick church closed in 1956. There was even talk of turning it into a house, but plans came to nothing, and then like the Phoenix, it rose again and was reopened on May 23rd 1965.

Now in the year 2000 except for Christmas and the Harvest Festival, the congregation of Fritham Free Church United is small for the twice monthly service, but the church is there to serve those in the village who wish to worship there, or cannot get to the parish church, St Peters in Bramshaw. The annual collection round the village for Harvest, once undertaken by horse and cart is now carried out by car. The Harvest Service is one opportunity for neighbours to meet neighbours and exchange a few words, instead of the more usual wave from a car.

The upkeep of the fabric of this building is very important to the Trustees, and with the ever willing and generous help from the villagers, the church is in excellent condition. Some improvements may take longer than others of course, and in 1966 it was decided that plans for a toilet would be put in hand. This was finished 32 years later in 1998, which just goes to prove that ‘though the mills of God grind exceeding small...’ we get there in the end.

For many years the lovely old organ in the church was of the ‘pedal and puff’ era, and played for years by May Meech. It was a regular occurrence after a service for May and Stan, who was church secretary, and the congregation, to stay behind and enjoy an impromptu singsong. Although they were then living 15 miles away in Ringwood, they returned to Fritham every week. As a boy Stan Meech had lived behind the church in Meeches Farm and May was the girl next door.

In the last few years, the regular organist, Vikki Willis a young housewife had been pedalling furiously uphill for years. Then like the organist in the old song, in 1982 a stranger who had been camping in the Forest, dropped in for the service and stayed behind afterwards to look at the organ.

“May I play it?” he asked. He adjusted stops which hadn’t been touched for years and with a flurry of pumping, he began to play and the astonished congregation thought they had been transported to Westminster Abbey and the Royal Albert Hall rolled into one. It was obvious that their young organist could not produce such wonderful volume without first attending a body building course, but the stranger explained the mysteries of modern technology, in the form of an electric pump. An organ fund was started, and within weeks, thanks to the ever generous help from the village, the old organ was rejuvenated. And the stranger? He was never seen again!

There is a Roll of Honour of the first World War, a plaque describing the great Christian involvement of the Schultze Gunpowder Factory, and a few plaques on the wall, remembering past servants of the church, but one which draws most comment is the memorial to the four young men of the village, three of them brothers, who perished aboard the Titanic. A fifth young man, Charles Bellamy, my father, was due to go with his friends, but had to cancel at the last minute due to family illness. He waved them goodbye at Southampton, promising to join them the next week, and one can only imagine his and the village’s anguish when the news of the disaster reached them.

A few years ago, in 1982, this memorial plaque nearly claimed its own victims. There had been an Open Day in the church with a photograph exhibition, and for the last hour Mrs Edith Winter had been resting in the pew underneath the plaque, nursing her youngest granddaughter Tina. As the last visitor left, and the door slammed, it was noticed that the plaque was slowly moving away from the wall. Just in time, willing hands supported the plaque until help arrived, and the heavy stone was taken down, and sent away to be restored.

Relatives of the boys were located and contacted, and invited to attend a service of dedication when the plaque was replaced, and a very moving meeting of strangers, and reunion of scattered families took place. These young men are not forgotten, and the Titanic will always be linked to Fritham Free Church and the history of Fritham.

Fritham National CE School 1862 - 1928

When the Eyre Family settled in the locality in 1798, Fritham and Bramshaw children reaped the benefit of George Briscoe Eyre's paternalistic attitude towards his workers and their children. The Bramshaw Boys School was registered in 1811 and the girls followed in 1819. However, Elizabeth Merson (1979) suggests Mr. Briscoe Eyre did not support a separate school for Fritham children. Many years later Mr. G.E. Briscoe Eyre outlined the reasons for his disapproval in his letter to the Director of Education dated 29.6.1909:

> *'The setting up of a regular school in the Chapel at Fritham is a luxury rather than a necessity. I tried to save the Parish this expense, the Fritham children having always been the most regular and satisfactory of those attending Bramshaw Schools.'*

This was quite an achievement for the children of Fritham, given the long walk they had to undertake daily.

It is probable that in keeping with the beliefs of the times, only religious instruction and needlework were taught, so that the children would grow up to become decorous, moral and useful in the station 'wherein they had been placed by Providence'. Gradually, however, it was considered wise to teach reading and writing, and thus the gap slowly closed between the education of the sons and daughters of the wealthy and the children of the labourers. The village children, however, were expected to help on the farms and smallholdings, and during the busy times of the year such as harvest, school took second place, and as a consequence their education suffered. It was therefore, a great step forward when in 1862 it was decided to start a school in Fritham which would also serve as a Chapel-at-Ease.

Alan Broderick, the vicar was the prime mover in establishing a Fritham School. The arrival of the Schultze Factory increased the population of Fritham and this fact may have added weight to Mr. Broderick's plans. Albert Winter who was born in 1840, remembers hearing the school bell ringing for the first time when he was working in the fields of Fritham in 1866.

The little school, on the plain leading to Stoney Cross, was given into the care of the vicar and three gentlemen, Henry Compton, Eustace Heathcote and Thomas Rowlinson, who together with three Christian ladies and churchwardens, managed the organisation. The schoolroom was 30 feet long by 15 feet wide and 17 feet high. A wood burning stove provided heating during the colder months of the year. The principal teacher was required to keep a logbook, which may have been a chore for the teacher concerned but the logs have provided a rich source of information for present day villagers. The village children were taught the three 'R's', general subjects and singing. At the time of opening thirty two to thirty five pupils attended the school. Full attendance was reliant on a number of factors the main one being the weather. Wet weather resulted in poor attendance, possibly due to many pupils having unsuitable footwear and in some cases no footwear. Harvest time and the period after the harvest holiday from August to September also resulted in irregular attendance.

16. Fritham School circa 1920

Pupils experienced a number of official and unofficial holidays. A 'smoking' stove and the sweeping of the chimney resulted in a half-day holiday. Sunday school and chapel treats also provided a holiday from school. During the summer holidays the pupils attended the annual tea given by the Eyre family at Warrens in Bramshaw. This school treat was very popular with the pupils and their accompanying parents. The parents wandered around the garden admiring the shrubs and flowers while the children ran races and played games under the eye of their teacher.

The teacher's log book of 1887 records the result of a school inspection and reflects a familiar concern a century later:

'Her Majesty's Inspector is unable to recommend the payment of any

merit grant on the present occasion due to seriously defective spelling and arithmetic.'

In 1889 the school was closed by the managers resulting in the elder boys and girls walking to Bramshaw Village School. In January 1890 Fritham School opened for infants and older girls only. Only a month later the teaching, especially the discipline, was unsatisfactory resulting in the dismissal of the present teacher.

By 1911 the pupils of Fritham achieved a more favourable report from Her Majesty's Inspector:

'This small school is making steady progress. The children are in good order and they are more interested in their work.'

The inspector's recommendation following this positive statement may not seem appropriate to the present day children of Fritham:

'Owing to the remoteness of the neighbourhood which the school serves, particular attention should be paid to the training of the children's speech and the development of their powers of self expression'.

However, the pupils began to expand their horizons in 1913 when they attended a Music Festival in Southampton and took a day trip to Bournemouth. Miss Henderson from Fritham Lodge and Miss Majorie Eyre were frequent visitors to the school 'superintending' the writing of essays and checking up on the general progress of the pupils.

The well-worn piece of blotting paper lying opposite the entry in the teacher's log books on the 27th. July 1928 records the last day of the school's existence, a school that often prompted visiting inspectors to comment on its unique location:

'Nothing could be pleasanter than the cheerful, friendly air of this remote school.....the managers and local residents show a real and genuine interest in the school...' *(Miss Collins HMI 1922)*

A former villager, Alf Batten, remembers as a boy receiving sixpence for carrying out the daily job of ringing the school bell before attending school himself. The school building was also used as a church so he was also entrusted with taking up the collection, closely watched by the Vicar! One Sunday there was a christening and he was asked to get a jug of water for it (at that time he thought the water came from the River Jordan!). He could not get the water pump in the lobby area to work, so he collected enough from a puddle outside the school! *Close inspection of the photograph of Fritham School taken around the 1920's, reveals the bell on the front apex of the roof.*

Alf remained at the school with his school friend Norman Winter until he was ten years old, when he inherited his brother's bike to cycle to Bramshaw Boy's School.

The school building was later converted into an Art Studio by Peter Bright (working for Turner and Stevens Building Firm, Lyndhurst). The studio was for Sir Timothy Eden to paint and provide storage for his paintings.

Our Pub by Hugh Pasmore

There are at least three 'Royal Oak' pubs in the Forest, but to me there will never be one to equal our 'Fritham Oak' with its long history stretching back into the days when Cromwell was ravaging the country.

Over the centuries there have been many books in which reference is made to the village of Fritham and in the majority there is allusion to the hostelry or alehouse. Deeper investigation by way of the deeds of the property reveal that in October 1677 John Emblyn senior granted a 1000 year lease to Joseph Emblyn, after which nothing comes to light until 1853 when a spinster, Anna Maria Biddle takes over the lease by way of a £1500 mortgage on which she agrees to pay 5% per annum; in 1866 this devolves to William Jefferies and on his demise the property was sold in lots by auction. The Inn was then bought by William Morgan Benett who lived at Fritham House, Benett was in the legal profession and his history is recorded elsewhere in this book. He died in 1891 leaving the Royal Oak to his wife Barbara, who in turn left it to her son William Charles when she died in 1894. Two years later he sold the holding comprising the pub and 4.3 acres to David Faber, a partner in the Brewers, Strong & Co. of Romsey for £1463.5.0. Strongs retained it until 1994 when it was transferred to Andrew & Eileen Taylor, the sitting tenants.

The Taylor family first came to the pub in 1909 when Bert Taylor's father took over the licence from a Mr. G. Gear, the outgoing licensee, on September 30th, paying his predecessor the sum of £23.6s 0d for a wide variety of equipment including 6 spittoons, one straight pint, nine lip pints, five lip quarts and four various glasses.

My first visit to the Royal Oak was in 1932 when I moved to Fritham, and now in my nineties I can still recall the magic of those days. There were of course cars that brought 'foreigners' (known as 'groccles' by the locals) to the pub but car ownership then was not universal and traffic was but a tithe of todays mad rush. Prior to the 1939 war and in fact for some years after, the lunchtime clients were largely local farm or local Forest workers.

At that time the front bar was divided into two by a wall running parallel to the road and stretching from the bar to the opposite wall. This formed a kitchen in which the housewife not only served both front and back bars but also did the household cooking. The locals took over the back bar, entering by the side door, leaving the front bar for the groccles. Some years after the war this dividing wall was removed, exposing the large wood-burning fire for the customers.

The back bar had a fascinating atmosphere, being the regular haunt of Forest Keepers and other Forest workers as well as the farming fraternity. A few names which spring to mind are Jack Humby, Gilbert Smith and Alistair Holloway all Forest Keepers, Bill Loader, landlord of the Foresters Arms at Gorley, Agister and Verderer Gerald Forward (a legend in the Forest), followed a little later by the irrepressible Colonel Valery Le Marchant, his bailiff Charles Sillence, and Jim Soffe the village thatcher, who much enjoyed his beer and frequent arguments. Sadly all but one have now departed this life.

After the Second World War broke out in 1939 there was a gradual exodus of villagers as they joined the fighting forces and it was six long years before I frequented the 'Oak' again.

In the back parlour was (and still is) a large open fireplace with a huge chimney in which it is possible to stand upright. Every year Bert would 'smoke' half a pig in the flue with its head just out of view and it was routine when a newcomer lady ventured into the 'sacred' haunt, to encourage her to look up the chimney, resulting inevitably in a terrified scream as she came face to face with the hanging pig!

In 1961 Sir Oliver Crosthwaite-Eyre M.P., commenced negotiations with a view to introducing a Parliamentary Bill involving the Bramshaw Commons and as he was already an occasional visitor to the pub it seemed an appropriate place to consort with the affected commoners. Lady Crosthwaite-Eyre sometimes accompanied him and these conferences were flippantly termed 'The New Forest Parliament'! They certainly were convivial affairs and achieved much in the way of compromises when the Commoners claimed their rights were being unduly curtailed by the restrictions proposed in the 1964 Act of Parliament. This act was instigated by Sir Oliver Crosthwaite-Eyre.

New Year's Eve at the 'Oak' was traditional and things became very merry as midnight approached. On the stroke of twelve Bert would sing 'To Be a Farmers Boy'. In those days we had little trouble from the 'law' and apart from sometimes forgetting when closing time arrived we gave no reason for interference.

We were fortunate indeed that on Bert's death, his son Andrew took over for Andrew was almost a replica of his father, a real Forester and farmer and he was sadly missed when he moved to a large farm in Somerset.

When it became known that Andrew was leaving in 1998 there was much concern in the village as to the future of the Royal Oak. It had been little altered for almost a century and it was feared the new owner might press for modernisation and enlargement entirely out of keeping. It was with some relief therefore that we learned that Clive Bowring and his sister Julie who already lived in the village were the new joint owners. In the event the modernisation has been done with considerable taste and much of the old charm which I knew 65 years ago still remains. The licensees who now run the pub are Fritham villagers Neil and Pauline McCulloch.

What I wonder will our pub be like at the end of the next 65 years!

Fritham House by Margaret Houlgate

This imposing house, now a nursing home, which stands at the entrance to the village has seen a great many structural changes, and has been home to many different families over the years. One such family's occupation has been well documented in a diary kept by the family.

In April 1861, William Morgan Benett, a successful London barrister living in Regent's Park, came to Fritham to see Fritham House, or Cottage as it was called. It had been advertised to let, and William thought it would be suitable as a country cottage for his large family, providing it could be put in order. He took the property on a lease, and on the last day of June Mrs Benett, her daughter Margaret, son John and nanny Maria, together with two young children Annie and Newton and their nursemaid Ann, came down to the Forest.

At the time the house was occupied by an 'aged women' named Jenny Windebank and her daughter-in-law, Mary, who were 'not really prepared for visitors'. According to Mrs Benett the house was in a very dirty condition, there were no chairs suitable for sitting on, and the food was not at all appetising and comprised 'a bit of mutton, bread and butter and tea'. Jenny Windebank said that the teapot was a very nice one, but leaked somewhat and the rickety two-pronged forks and the two uncleanable leaded spoons were the only cutlery in the house.

Mrs Benett writes, "Still we solaced ourselves with strawberries from the garden, and delicious cream from a neighbouring farm, and as Maria had her nursery possessions, we soon got the two spoons and forks between us three 'in the parlour'.

"At first nanny contemplated packing up and returning to town immediately, but even she was conquered by the extreme beauty of the situation, the lovely clean air, and the indescribable clutter of muddle.

"We were obliged to work hard all day, and seldom sat down except at meal times. We found a little bacon, and plenty of green peas agrowing, potatoes, not to be despised, and never were we so merry and hearty in our lives. Jenny was a character, the wittiest old creature possible, and the house walls resounded with laughter from morning until night. At night our labours increased as the spiders requiring to be killed cannot be numbered.

"After a day or two we were joined by Willie, and in a week by all the rest of the family, (at least ten) who arrived at Totton station, and were met by a neighbour Mr Rawlinson, who kindly drove some to Fritham in his pony and trap, while the rest of the family followed in a fly."

Three weeks after moving into Fritham House, daughter Barbara started her diary of life in the country in 1861 and the following few years, and we are now able to gently turn a few pages of the past and look into a bygone age. Barbara writes:

"For weeks the house continued under the domination of painters, paperers and varnishers, then when we fancied things were coming to a finish, a grate would drop out or a door refuse to do anything. Then the rain poured through the thatched roof and spoilt the new paper. In late September we began an entire new slated roof which came to a successful end in November, this after a good deal of excitement when, for instance, the rain came in on our heads in torrents and Maria and I were then up for hours in the night, rushing all over the house armed with basins and old carpets to withstand the enemy.

"However, no one came to any grief and by December we were pretty comfortably settled and all the children thrived as we could wish. Dear little Anne and Newton remain as they have been for some time, and although very happy in their new quarters, do not improve in health."

During the following months the Benett family settled in and made friends with their neighbours, mentioning Mr and Mrs Gradbourne of Lyburn, the Heathcotes, Mr Broderick the vicar and Mr Eyre. For transport the family had a wagonette and a little four-wheeled chaise, drawn by Moonraker, so named by Papa Benett (who came to Fritham most week-ends,) 'because he comes from Wiltshire'. Mr Benett looking for more ponies for the family, bought a chestnut and a fourteen hand handsome grey pony, both animals belonged to Landery, the brother-in-law of the Benett's washer woman. It wasn't long before both ponies were in harness and on the 27th of July we read that Margaret was riding Peggy, and papa was on the grey. Willie had to use Shanks's Pony, however, when he set off to walk the eight miles to Totton, on his journey to the Isle of Wight to visit friends.

Life at Fritham House in 1861 was taken up with walks, reading, making things for fancy fairs and visiting friends and neighbours. Friends were entertained to dinner regularly, and the evening always ended with singing round the piano. Entertainment was home made with the children playing charades, singing and dancing, and cards were also a popular pastime.

It was common practice to walk to Totton, Brook and of course, Bramshaw Church. 'It is such a pretty walk through the Forest'. Picnics were very popular and on one occasion they took bacon, eggs, potatoes, apples, bread and butter and made a fire in the Forest and fried the eggs and bacon and cooked the potatoes in the ashes. 'Everything did taste so nice'.

Son Willie, had an extended and probably unwelcome holiday that first summer in 1861 when he called for a short visit with his parents and siblings and was then laid up with serious boils on his foot and ankle and he had to remain in Fritham for the rest of the school break.

In November of that first year, daughter Barbara notes in her diary that new people with four year old Henry had moved into Fritham Lodge. 'The Phillips are much pleasanter neighbours than the Browns!'

Mrs Benett does appear to have been a lady who liked to get things moving, because as well as coming to a problem cottage, and then organising the extensive repairs, and being surrounded by a number of children, she arranged for the setting up of a little Sunday School in the kitchen. Barbara, the eldest daughter, taught the bigger boys, Margaret took the big girls and Edith the little boys. That first Christmas the Benetts gave all the school children and their mothers a tea, and a Christmas tree and this was apparently considered a great success.

A new chapel was planned at the other end of the village, and until it was completed there was talk of holding evening services in Mrs Thorn's barn but as the family would soon have to return to London, nothing was decided.

The family enjoyed Christmas in Fritham, and then on 13th January Mr and Mrs Benett returned to their London home, leaving four children and a maid at Fritham House. After a few more days, before leaving Fritham and joining their parents in London, the children walked round the village saying goodbye to old Mrs Spratt, Mrs Henbest, Mrs Thorn, Mrs Goddon, all the school children and all the animals. When they said goodbye to the Bradburnes, these friends promised to visit the Benetts in London during the great exhibition at the Crystal Palace.

It was four months later in May 1862 that the family gathered again at Fritham House and looked forward to another summer in the country, but according to daughter Barbara's diary, the holiday didn't start off too well with news that frail little Annie was not well at all, the weather was wet and Mr Broderick preached the 'most stupid sermon'. Even the Sunday school children were troublesome with Jimmy Spratt making a noise and disturbing the whole school, then falling fast asleep and sleeping for the rest of the time. Nor was the cricket game in the evening a success, when Willie and his friends hit a cricket ball and accidentally killed a duck.

In August of 1862, the school chapel was opened by the Bishop, and the occasion was marked with a lunch and a large party.

After this date, the news of the Benett family is rather sparse, but in May 1863, her Diary notes that Mrs Benett was sent for from Fritham to return to London at once where 'after a short illness, our dear little Annie was relieved from her life of misery and suffering. We all felt this was a matter for sincere thankfulness and her new face, restored by death to more than her original beauty and sweetness was a great comfort to me'.

In 1864 the two elder daughters Barbara and Margaret 'came out' with a very gay season and when they returned to Fritham for the summer they found they had new neighbours again at Fritham Lodge, a Mrs Lewis and her family. Mrs Benett had taken new servants with her this summer, a cook and a butler and Fanny, a kitchen maid-all. But Fanny had to be sent away at a day's notice, it appears, in consequence of a quarrel with Mr Broderick, he of the 'stupid sermon'. Oh dear, one can only wonder!

And then after a few notes in 1870, when it is briefly reported that daughter Sarah and her brother Newton 'begin to farm in earnest in November', news of the fortunes of this Victorian family peters out, and a new family takes over Fritham House.

Fritham House was sold in 1891, the year papa Benett died, and it was bought by Doctor Chapman, whose son captained England at cricket. Doctor Chapman ran it as a boys' school until 1910, when it was sold again, this time to Daniel Hanbury.

Hanbury pulled down the much smaller house, and proceeded to build the present house on the same site with stables, laundry, a poultry unit and staff quarters. He added to the property all the nearby land that he could buy. Eventually Fritham House comprised of all the land surrounded by the two roads leading to the village, except for four cottages along the edge, but Moor Cottage belonged to him.

Hanbury was determined to create an imposing property, reputedly as a wedding present for his daughter, but he sold it before it was completed to one Henry Stafford Northcote in 1914. It is noted that the house was originally sold to 'trustees for HSN a person of unsound mind'. He later recovered and the house handed over to him, and he proceeded to live there until about 1921.

In order to produce a really worthwhile house and stable block, he equipped it with electric light, the electricity being generated by diesel engines housed in Lister Cottage, (hence its appellation by the writer), and he wanted the whole property served by an elaborate water supply provided from the water tower, and piped from there to the house and the stable block. Several springs which fed the stream running through the side of the village emanated in the sloping field near the village and these were ducted into an enormous underground tank holding nearly 200,000 gallons of water which lies between the two sprinklers of the sewage plant. The little brick hut nearby used to house the electric pump (connected to Lister Cottage), which pumped the water into the 5000 gallon tank at the top of the water tower; thus there is about 400 yards of lead piping and the same amount of heavy multicore copper cable underground between those two.

During the war, when the Stoney Cross aerodrome was created, a water supply was laid on that was extended into the village soon afterwards; as it was obviously a great advantage this was then connected up to the water tower and now supplies it. The Water Company had to install a special pump beside the water tower on the old aerodrome to boost the water up to the Fritham House water tower, about eighty feet higher.

Fritham Lodge by Margaret Houlgate

A great deal has happened at Fritham Lodge during the last 368 years; Royalty has lodged there, many people have lived under its roof, rumours, scandals and myths have grown up around this great house, but actual documentation is rare, and it is not easy to sort fact from fiction.

The first mention of Fritham Lodge is in 1631 when John Chamberlayne of Lyndhurst was granted a cottage with garden, woodland and an adjacent 5 acres called Crowders in Fritham, a property worth 6d a year. Did he live there alone, with a family, or did he have a lodger? We do know that one Nicholas Lawes, an underforester, was resident at the house in 1634, when according to the archives in Winchester, he was fined for cutting wood for browsing in Eyeworth Woods.

However more pressing problems were to arrive for John Chamberlayne in 1634, when he received instructions from the Chief Justice ‘to build stables and lodgings for the accommodation of his majesties attendants ... as may be fit and requisite to receive and entertain and lodge his majesties train’.

One could speculate that John had been granted the cottage in Fritham in the first place, in order that he would be there to oversee the building of the new house when the time came.

The house, which was to be used as a hunting lodge for King Charles I, was built in 1635, the exact location may have been on the present site of Fritham Lodge or on the site of Crowders cottage. A fireback dug out of an old fireplace during restoration work by the present owners Chris and Rosie Powell, bore Charles I's coat of arms and the date 1635. The excitement of being able to prove historical rumours quickly evaporated, however, when it was discovered that identical firebacks can be bought at an enterprising forge at Kings Worthy near Winchester. Authentic or not, the fireback is now set into the wall high at the front of the house for all to see and ponder on.

Legends have a habit of leading us up the garden path into a blank wall, and another disappointment for the new owners in 1985 was the exploration of a secret passage which was rumoured to run from Fritham Lodge to the Royal Oak. Hopes and excitement were high when builders dug up a man sized old brick tunnel running from the house towards the pub. Unfortunately, it petered out after about 50 yards! What, one wonders is the story behind that abandoned project? One suggestion is that it was used for holding water in times of drought.

Arthur Oxford's name crops up in the records in 1634 and also appears on the Swainmote for Fritham in the 1660's. This gentleman appears to have been a man of substance by 1686 who, with William Oxford owned Fritham Lodge, and let it out to K. Barrow for the sum of 4 shillings a year.

For the next 80 years, little is known about this old house and its occupants, although there are tales to suggest Charles II gave it to one of his mistresses. Without records, we can only speculate.

Records help us briefly again in 1783 when according to a book 'A Hunting Pageant', 22 year old Mr Harbin, who was the founder of the New Forest Hunt, was living at Fritham Lodge. Mr Harbin died in 1837 aged 76 and his obituary said: " ...though a regular welter (about 20 stone) he stood up in his stirrups, and rode with the activity of a 10 stone man. The New Forest is admitted on all hands to be an awkward country to get across, yet being perfectly acquainted with its every nook, he generally contrived to be up at 'who-whoop'. In private life he combined the socialities of the old English Gentleman with the hospitality of the sportsman." Obviously one of Fritham's characters.

Thirteen years after Mr Harbin's death, Fritham Lodge was in the hands of the Heathcote family, and a scandal rocked Fritham. First Lieutenant Edmund Heathcote was away at sea for a three year period leaving his wife at home, and she conceived a child which was born just after the return of her husband. Not a happy homecoming! Divorce in 1850 was not usual or easy, requiring an Act of Parliament, and a copy of this divorce is held by the present owners of the Lodge. It is said that "a navy man" who lived in the house in the nineteenth century would watch the ships in Southampton water through his telescope in the days before Linwood Copse had grown up to obscure the view.

Twenty six years after the scandal of the divorce, the house was bought by another hunting man, Master of the New Forest Foxhounds, Sir Reginald Graham. Sir Reginald and his wife lived happily in Fritham and brought a quieter period to the history of the house as he writes in his book 'Fox Hunting Recollections', "Up to 1876 I had resided my bachelor days at Jessamine Cottage, Lyndhurst, but the 24th July in that year was the commencement of a happy life for me in double harness. We moved that summer to Fritham Lodge, two or three miles north of Stoney Cross, a charming spot on high ground, with views all over the Forest". Three years after moving in Sir Reginald added the dining room and passage.

Over the years the house itself has grown, first with two large Georgian wings, and then the addition in 1879 of a dining room and five foot passage through the cellar. It is recorded that the cost of this Victorian work was £150 with a £1 fine for every day the builder failed to meet the agreed completion day. It is interesting to note that the three major periods of its growth are clear from the height of the ceilings. Low ceilings in the early kitchen and middle part, high ceilings in the Georgian wings and in between for the later Victorian additions at the top of the house.

After the First World War, the Lodge was sold to the Henderson family for £2125. The Hendersons were a clerical family and the Very Reverend Edward Henderson was the Bishop of Wells. When the Bishop died in 1947, the house was sold for £2,750 to a Major Crane, who used the land for breeding pigs. This project in the difficult post-war, post-army years lasted a short 5 years before the house once again changed hands in 1952 and Mr and Mrs Jonas bought Fritham Lodge for £5,100.

Mrs Jonas bred racehorses and was the sister of Colonel Valery le Marchant of Fritham Farm. The Colonel owned the national favourite, The Ghost. The name was most appropriate for a horse that was sired by a stallion called Spiritus. Excitement was high in Fritham and villagers were very proud to have their own racehorse, quite apart from the good chance of sharing in the winnings on the day of the great race. The village was stunned and shocked therefore, when shortly before the race, this beautiful animal was killed in a road accident in Stockbridge. The Ghost was returning from exercise at the time.

17. The Meet at Fritham Lodge in 1957

The Jonas' occupation of 27 years at the Lodge was one of the longest in recent times when 5 years seemed to be normal. And when the next owner John Kirkpatrick, Master of the Buckhounds, bought the house at Auction in 1979, he and his family were to stay in Fritham for only 5 years.

The present (2000) owners Chris and Rosie Powell and their family have been in Fritham and part of the community since 1985, opening their garden to the public and holding the annual Church Fete in their lovely grounds. When John Chamberlayne was ordered in 1634 to build a house for a King surely he could not have imagined that as Fritham moves into the millennium, Fritham Lodge would still be a very important part of the village.

The Schultze Gunpowder Factory by Margaret Houlgate

Life in Fritham changed dramatically in the late 1800's when, after years of negotiation, false starts and objections from Commoners, a Mr Drayson began to establish a gunpowder manufactory at Eyeworth. Approximately seven years later he assigned the lease to a Mr Broderick but remained within the business. A few years later Drayson absconded incurring financial losses and Broderick assigned the lease to Messrs. Dale and Bailey for the Schultze Gunpowder Company.

A large reservoir was constructed to supply the huge amount of water necessary for the manufacturing process and over 100 years later, this 'lake' is a very popular tourist attraction drawing many visitors throughout the year.

Sixty large buildings, including shooting galleries and laboratories sprang up, as well as stabling for 40 horses. Grass tracks, unchanged for decades, were strengthened with forest gravel and huge carts, drawn by teams of heavy horses, trundled down the once quiet lanes. When full zinc lined containers proved too heavy for the horses to pull up the hill, a new road was cut through the Forest from Eyeworth to the Cadnam/Fordingbridge Road and this became known as Powder Mill Road. The rough track is still there to-day, but closed to traffic.

Houses were built for the workers, both in Eyeworth and Fritham and many Fritham villagers worked in the factory. Other workers, men and women thought nothing of walking 6 or more miles from surrounding villages every morning to start work at 6 a.m. and making the return journey at the end of the day. Workers could get up to £1.00 a week, compared with the agricultural wage of 12 shillings, and that extra money meant a great deal, and was worth the long walk every day.

These were hard days and the Company endeavoured to offer light relief, by arranging outings and organising The Band. The Band comprised of excellent and enthusiastic musicians and was in great demand throughout the district, where in their smart uniforms, they played for various functions, and gave concerts in village halls. They played regularly for the folk of Fritham and their repertoire included a good range of songs and sketches.

18. The Band from the Powder Mill

Even the little tin chapel benefited from this great company when it was 'adopted' by the factory owners, who erected a handsome brick building, with the help of the villagers' contributions. After the First World War, the great Schultze Gunpowder Factory was absorbed by the mighty ICI and closed with the loss of over 100 jobs. The new road was fenced off, the Forest closed ranks again and Fritham returned to its sleepy isolated existence.

For further reading, the history of this great company is meticulously recorded in a booklet 'New Forest Explosives' by Anthony Pasmore, published by The New Forest Section of the Hampshire Field Club in 1993.

Eyeworth Lodge by Hugh Pasmore

Fritham possesses three 'principal' houses - Fritham Lodge, Fritham House and Eyeworth Lodge. Of these the first two have already been documented in this chapter.

Eyeworth Lodge as a building does not claim any antiquity though it was built in Victorian times on a site very close to one of the old Forest keepers' cottages at Eyeworth. This was sited on the Eyeworth estate and in 1855 it is recorded as being in a somewhat dilapidated condition with its enclosure fences completely demolished, allowing the forest animals to graze right up to the cottage walls. It was in this year that the Forest keeper, George Cooper who as the Crown tenant, retired and Deputy Surveyor, Cumberbatch, assessed a rent at which the Crown offered the property for letting. A lease was then granted to a Mr Joseph Scorey, an innkeeper from Berkeley Square, London but this gentleman only lasted for three years and his executors surrendered the lease.

Shortly afterwards, in 1861, a Mr. Drayson appeared and negotiated a lease of £1500 on the property. In 1866 Drayson took a Mr. Broderick of London into partnership with a view to enlarging the gunpowder factory, but in 1869 he absconded, much to the chagrin of his deserted partner Mr Broderick. However this gentleman in turn assigned his lease to Messers Date & Bailey of the Schultze Gunpowder Factory and Captain Schultze was a major force in the expansion of the factory though he does not appear actually to be a partner in the firm.

In 1883 when the factory was fully established Mr. R.S.W. Griffiths appears and seems to have been a potent force in the company. It was Mr Griffiths, a well respected local personage, who apparently built Eyeworth Lodge in typical Victorian design of brick with tiled roof, an imposing property which has been modernised and enlarged within the past decade.

CHAPTER SIX

Fritham Voices

Finally, as we reach the end of the twentieth century some of our present day inhabitants write about Fritham past, present and future.

"We thought we had got to know the Forest quite well over the years, and had been looking for a base for some time. We weren't in a hurry, but wanted to find the 'right' place. Saturdays were often spent looking in Estate Agents' windows in Lymington or Lyndhurst.

"One beautiful late spring morning, we spotted a cottage for sale in Fritham. Fritham? Where was that? In we went, collected the details and set off. Rather to our surprise, we found ourselves heading north. We had thought the Forest boundary wasn't far north of Cadnam, but the directions said carry on after the roundabout...north. Climbing a long and heavily wooded hill, it seemed as if we were heading for the North Pole.

19. Views of Fritham from an old picture post card

"Suddenly we were out into the sunshine and the open Forest. A left turn and we were already intrigued. Wonderful views to the right and woods to the left. Then another signpost. Following this we reached a full stop. No Through Road. Could that be right? We ventured on with increasing anticipation down into a shallow valley. Up the other side and a lovely old thatched pub. A green with ponies and a few pigs. We were nearly there and getting excited. A few moments more and we saw it. Without leaving the car, we looked at each other. 'That's it,' we said simultaneously....and four weeks later we bought it."

"Fritham when I came in 1980 turned out to be everything I expected it to be. I was left in peace to carry on with my own affairs and those people I met were affable, helpful and in particular thirsty, thank God. The cows were universally well disposed and have become even more so. By and large this atmosphere has continued."

"On returning to the village after an absence of many years, the first impression was how untidy the village is now. Twenty-five years ago Fritham was almost self supporting with a shop, visiting butcher, fishmonger and travelling shop. Now there is only a milkman, a dustcart and the travelling library every two weeks. People are friendly when they meet, but seldom meet these days."

"Living in Fritham is a great privilege which we are lucky enough to have enjoyed for eleven years so far and we hope to continue to enjoy for years to come.

"We have seen many changes during our time here but the main elements of camaraderie and kindness remain unchanged.

"Having B & B guests has given us a wide experience of mankind from many different countries, all of whom seem to appreciate our lovely surroundings with its wealth of wildlife. A recent couple from Denmark asked to have their BBQ in a field. When they returned to the house some time later, we asked if they had seen any deer as we had been plagued by a large number throughout the summer. When they replied 'No' we expressed surprise but they insisted they had seen no wild deer, 'Just your breeding herd' ......such are the joys of living in Fritham."

"Fifteen years have passed by like the blink of an eye - where did it go? I moved into my cottage with my youngest son and my Alsatian in 1984. There was a lot to do - the laurel hedge encroached six feet over the lawn and clearing old leaves was a daily chore. In 1986 I was bitten by an adder, so the hedge came out along the driveway and a brick wall frontage was built. This caused a commotion and earned the name the 'Great Wall of China'.

"From my position, with the kitchen facing my garage, I don't see a lot of what is going on so it is pretty quiet. I get most of the news from my nearby neighbour. Things are very peaceful, it is lovely here. I wonder what the year 2000 will bring? Peace and happiness to all of us in Fritham I hope. Maybe I will start writing my book!"

"We first saw our house in Fritham on a very wet Whitsun weekend in May 1984 (should have been warned about the weather then) and moved in quickly the following August. This was a complete dream for me as having been born and bred in Lyndhurst and brought up in Ashurst I was very keen to move from our house in Hythe to the real Forest!

"We met our nearest neighbours very soon and made contact with Dave - the 'paper boy' as we called him. It became apparent after a while (via Dave and Albert) that we were the focus of some village gossip as having bought the first house in the village to be put up for sale for £100,000 - unheard of for a house of our size in those days. The other rumour came to our ears after our first very cold snowy winter when people kept asking when we would be moving as they had heard that we couldn't stand the extreme weather conditions in Fritham. Needless to say we had a good chuckle as neither tale was true (although living on top of a hill in January 1990 when our stables blew away in winds of over 100 mph definitely gave us cause to dislike the winter weather!).

"Fifteen years later we both think it is the best place to live in the Forest and still marvel at the beautiful view, wonder where the 'Lock' is and enjoy all the country pursuits and gossip that go with life in a small village. I think the only downside to modern life in the Forest at large is the greater accessibility that the M3/M27 has given to many more thousands of tourists who flock in at weekends and bank holidays and clog up the roads of small villages such as ours and who seem to have very little consideration for the animals on the roads or the country way of life."

"We are relative newcomers to Fritham but have come to love it dearly and have been made to feel really part of the community which has not always been the case in other places. Yet, even in the short time we have been here there have been tremendous changes and Fritham has changed from a tranquil haven into a holiday resort in

20. Animals take priority on the roads in Fritham

many ways. This has mainly come about since the installation of the cycle track signs. We presumed the signs were intended for the use of people on their bicycles only and not, actually, intended to encourage cars with three and four bicycles strapped on the back to come rushing along the lanes. Let us hope that in some way we can retain the peacefulness of our village and allow the wild life the freedom to safely wander where they like as otherwise the whole ambience of Fritham will be changed for good and at a great loss to villagers."

"As you turn off the main Fordingbridge road and start the journey to Fritham you begin to get a sense of the uniqueness of this very special village. The dignified oak trees silently greet you as you wend your way past the ponies and cattle contentedly grazing the verges, the donkey family browsing the lanes and the pigs surrounding the old red telephone box. You can while away an endless amount of time gazing at the view that changes with each season. As you do so you will also share this pleasure with a group of fallow deer, the odd pheasant and occasionally a family of Canada Geese. Often in early Spring and Autumn a cloudy blustery day will give way to a calm sun filled evening when you can enjoy the rich colour and tranquillity of our village.

21. Pigs and piglet under the Oak Tree by the old red telephone box in Fritham

“Some years ago now, shortly after moving to Fritham I remember putting the customary name and address on the back of a cheque at a store a considerable distance from Fritham. The shop assistant on reading the address said ‘Oh you live in Fritham you are so lucky, I love going to Fritham.’ As time has passed I realised the true meaning of her comment. Most villagers who live in Fritham care passionately about the village and will vociferously safeguard their village and the surrounding Forest. Often in jest villagers have been known to suggest building a moat around Fritham to protect it. The sense of community is strong in the village with most villagers turning their hand to fund raising, celebrating a special event or helping a neighbour. We are fortunate to have a number of ‘wise’ villagers who, having lived in Fritham a considerable amount of time, enjoy sharing their knowledge of the village and Forest with more ‘recent’ villagers. In this way the past does inform the present. I only wish I had moved to Fritham sooner.....”

“It was my brother-in-law who told us about the house for sale, in Fritham. ‘Fritham,’ I said!! ‘Never heard of it,’ I said! ‘Has a great pub,’ he said ! ‘We’ll see the house, if we can go to the pub afterwards’ I said !!

Since then we have discovered that Fritham has much more to offer than ‘just a pub’. After a hectic working week it is a great place to relax. The countryside, the people, the peace, the walks and the animals, at all times outweigh the Sunday morning rush hours. Without car parks life would be complete. May Fritham be conserved for future generations.”

“As a new citizen dog in Fritham, I would like to write (like Dido) a few lines about dog life in Fritham. My friends Willow, Sparkie, Merlin, Holly, Suzie, Jazzie, Stig, Katie and Bruno have all urged me to get a dog-paw on or in this book. The dogs in Fritham have a good life, with so much opportunity for walks. It is sad though, to see both our owners and us get older and slower.

We dogs, do not want any changes in the village and look forward to long and happy lives full of smells, cats, other animal friends, lots of food and comfy beds in a village where time stands still.”

“Sometimes on a flight to America the planes go over Fritham, and you catch a glimpse of the village, a small circle of green fields surrounded on all sides by the wild heather and woods. This contrast is part of the joy of Fritham: the Englishness of the fields of sheep and horses, the Royal Oak and the red brick houses, but all around the endless moorland and Forest where you can walk or ride for miles and miles and see wonderful wildlife. To know that the almost unique way of life of commoning will continue and that the surrounding open Forest is totally protected from being built up makes it very special.”

APPENDIX I

FRITHAM VILLAGERS SERVING THEIR COUNTRY DURING THE SECOND WORLD WAR 1939 - 1945

Cecil Aston	RAF - Group Captain
Doreen Aston	WAF
Bert Coundley	RAF
Myrtle Coundley (Hickman)	Land Army
Walter Deacon	Army
Ted Gee	Royal Navy
Geoff Hickman	RAF
John Hickman	RAOC
Hugh Pasmore	Royal Artillery
Margaret Pasmore	ATS Transport
Doris Winter	NAAFI
Fred Winter	RAF

APPENDIX 2

VILLAGERS LIVING IN FRITHAM IN THE YEAR 2000
Taken from the Register of Electors 2000

Adlard, Christopher G.	The Old School House
Atkins, Catherine M.	Kings Garn, Fritham Court
Atkins, Henry J.	Kings Garn, Fritham Court
Beale, John H	The Gatehouse, Eyeworth
Beale, Marianne F.	The Gatehouse, Eyeworth
Beale, Rosalie C	The Gatehouse, Eyeworth
Beguin, Anne-Marie	Vale Cottage, Vale Farm
Bessant, Roland J	Coppice of Linwood
Blanchard, David	Fritham Court
Borelli, Amelia M	Amberwood Cottage
Bras, Isabelle	The Cottage, Fritham House
Bush, Dennis W	Quintons
Bush, Maureen E.	Quintons
Calais, Anne R	Dovecot
Calais, Henry G	Dovecot
Cassie, Alastair P.	Vale Cottage, Vale Farm
Clark, Ann T.	Woodlands
Creed, Timothy J	Longbeech Cottage
Daniels, Joyce I.	Cowpenn Cottage
Day, Michael L.	Buddles Corner
Day, Rose K.L.	Buddles Corner
Day, Sally J.	Buddles Corner
Day, William P.L.	Buddles Corner
Dibben, Alice M.	Janesmoor House
Dibben, Richard A.	Janesmoor House
Dominy, Charmian	Fritham Cottage
Dominy, John K.	Fritham Cottage
Dugmore, Bruce D.	Robin Hill
Dugmore, Daniel G.	Robin Hill
Dugmore, Elisabeth S	Robin Hill
Fallowfield, Elfrida C	Old Post Office Farm
Fallowfield, Richard G	Old Post Office Farm
Gardner, Nigel M	Whiteside Farm
Giddings, Brian A	Vale Cottage
Giddings, Iris M	Vale Cottage
Giddings, John	Ivylea
Giddings, Julia L	Ivylea
Giddings, Emily	Ivylea
Giddings, Jack	Ivylea
Hankinson, John	Fritham Farm
Hankinson, Penelope A	Fritham Farm
Harper, Angela M	The Old School House
Heinst, Johan S	Brinton House
Heinst, Marie B	Brinton House
Heinst, Nathalie M	Brinton House
Heinst, Carl R	Brinton House
Hickman, Derek A	Vale Farm
Holt, Brian C	Moor Farm
Houlgate, Clifford R	Valletta Cottage
Houlgate, Margaret E	Valletta Cottage
Jarvis, John M	Eyeworth Lodge
Keen, Christopher C	White House
Keen, Tamsyn E	White House
Keen, Thomas	White House
Keen, Eleanor	White House
Keen, James	White House
Loader, Ron	Ivy Cottage
McAdams, Brenda	Howen
McAdams,William	Howen
McCulloch, Neil	Meechers Farm
McCulloch, Pauline	Meechers Farm
McCulloch, Kathy	Meechers Farm
McCulloch, Jenna	Meechers Farm
Moody, Keith	Eyeworth Cottage
Munday,Teri S	1 Longcross Cottages
Munsey, Beverley	Armidale
Munsey, Geoffrey T	Armidale
Ng, Anthony	Studio Cottage
Ng, David	Studio Cottage
Ng, George	Studio Cottage
Ng, Stavroulla	Studio Cottage
Pack, Kathryn M	Locks View

Pack, Michael J	Locks View
Pasmore, Hugh C	North Bentley
Pasmore, Margaret E	North Bentley
Penfound, Barry G	Primrose Cottage
Penfound, Maureen	Primrose Cottage
Pilgrim, Kathleen N	Ivy Cottage
Pitcairn-Jones, Patricia J	Rose Cottage
Polack, Frances C	Clulbery Cottage
Poole, Susan	Eyeworth Cottage
Powell, Christopher	Fritham Lodge
Powell, Rosemary	Fritham Lodge
Powell, Ben N	Fritham Lodge
Powell, James A	Fritham Lodge
Powell, John C	Fritham Lodge
Powell, Lucy C	Fritham Lodge
Price, Margaret	Longbeech Cottage
Roche, Joyce K	Moor Cottage
Smith, Jacqueline A	Whiteside Farm
Spooner, Patricia M	The Garden Cottage
Stone, Louis W	Sandels
Stone, Maisie D	Sandels
Tanner, Philip J	2 Longcross Cottages
Thorne, Carolyn M	Bentley View
Thorne, Gordon H	Bentley View
Thorne,Thomas W	Bentley View
Twentyman, John	Mare&Foal Cottage
Twentyman, Valerie J	Mare&Foal Cottage
Whitby, Richard J	Homefield
Whitby, Margaret E	Homefield
Whitby, Jennifer	Homefield
Whitby, Catherine	Homefield
Whitcher, George	1 Longcross Cottages
Wier, Janet	Rose Cottage
Willis, Sylvia J	1 Church Villas
Willis, Benedict C	1 Church Villas
Winter, Edith K	Valetta House
Winter, Joyce K	Valetta House
Winter, Frederick W	2 Margarets Mead
Winter, Olive E	2 Margarets Mead
Winter, James	1 Margarets Mead
Winter, Susan	1 Margarets Mead
Winter, Jesse	1 Margarets Mead
Winter, Lee	1 Margarets Mead
Winter, Terence N	Supply Stores
Winter, Muriel	Supply Stores
Wood, Charles H.	Blackberry Farm
Wood, Fabia J.	Blackberry Farm
Wood, James W.	Blackberry Farm
Wood, Martin S.	Blackberry Farm
Wright, Derek B.	Fritham Grange
Wright, Sheila A.	Fritham Grange
Wylie, Judith R.	Powder Mill Farm, Eyeworth

Raymond Gale	Fritham Village Milkman
Gerald Wakeford	Fritham Village Postman

Fritham Free Church

Trustees:

Chairman	Mr. P. Bright
Secretary	Mrs. M. Winter
Treasurer	Mrs. M. Houlgate
	Mr. A. Winter
	Miss J. Winter
	Mrs. S. Willis
	Mr. D. Bush
	Mrs. M. Bush
	Dr. F. McAll
	Mr. K. McAll

BIBLIOGRAPHY

Brown, Alan 1996 *They Flew From The Forest* Published by Eon Graphics, Highcliffe

Census Returns 1891 Hampshire Records Office

Giles, Monica 1998 *Dio The Life of Dorothy Eyre and of Jack Crosthwaite her husband.* Published by Orphans Press, Leominster.

Kelly's Trade Directory 1859 Hampshire Records Office

Log Books of the principal teachers of Fritham National CE School 1885-1928 Hampshire Records Office

Lord Chief Justice in Eyre's Court c.1670 Published by Salisbury Benj. Cha. Collins and J. Johnson

Merson, Elizabeth. 1979 *Once there was The Village School* Paul Cave Publications.

Mays, J. O' Donald, 1989 *The New Forest Book, An Illustrated Anthology* New Forest Leaves

Pasmore, A. 1993 *New Forest Explosives* Published by the New Forest Section of Hampshire Field Club

Pasmore, H. 1991 *A New Forest Commoner Remembers.* New Forest Leaves

Pasmore, H and Heinst M. 1995 *Forest Reflections* Forest Views Publishing

Smith, Gilbert 1986 *Gilbert Smith Man of the New Forest.* Paul Cave Publications

Stagg, D.J. *New Forest Documents,* 1244-1334. 1979 Redwood Burns Ltd.

Stagg, D.J. *New Forest Documents 15th.- 17th.Centuries.* Alan Sutton Publishing Ltd.

Taylor, J. *Jesse Taylor's Diary* 1907-1923

INDEX